FUNDAMENTALS OF
PROFESSIONAL
FOOD PREPARATION

FUNDAMENTALS OF
PROFESSIONAL
FOOD PREPARATION

A Laboratory
Text-Workbook

DONALD V. LACONI
**Community and Technical College
The University of Akron**

John Wiley & Sons, Inc.
New York ▼ Chichester ▼ Brisbane ▼ Toronto ▼ Singapore

Library of Congress Cataloging in Publication Data:
Laconi, Donald V.
    Fundamentals of professional food preparation / Donald V. Laconi.
        p. cm.
    Includes bibliographical references.
    ISBN 0-471-59523-3 (pbk.)
    1. Quantity cookery. 2. Food service. I. Title.
TX820.L33 1995
641.5—dc20

Printed in the United States of America

10 9 8 7 6 5 4 3 2 1

Preface

My objective in writing this text-workbook was to create a learning tool for hospitality management, foodservice, or home economics students in a food production laboratory.

The book offers several benefits. Written in language that is straightforward and easy to understand, it provides basic information yet leaves the instructor free to organize the course and develop lectures without having to repeat a great majority of the reading material which is in the text. Recipes and formulas are broken down into logical steps that beginning students can follow easily.

All of the recipes have been tested, and the costs for the various preparations have been kept to a minimum, while allowing students the practice and experience they need. A *mise en place* sheet is provided on page 8 that can be duplicated for use with all recipes to organize the preparation work. The book also provides reference guides, charts, tables, glossaries of key terms with definitions, and 70 recipes in small quantities.

A survey of foodservice education programs indicates that in most institutions students are divided into several laboratory groups. Therefore, six different recipes or preparations are provided at the end of each lesson. This will save preparation time for instructors and also help ensure consistency in multiple course sections.

Preliminary drafts of the book were tested at the Community and Technical College, Hospitality Management Department at The University of Akron in the course entitled "Fundamentals of Food Preparation I: Skills and Basic Knowledge of Food Preparation Procedures in a Laboratory Situation." During the classroom testing, student evaluations were enormously valuable, and I thank my students and teaching assistants, present and past, for their contributions.

An instructor's manual is available, including topical outlines for every chapter, lesson plans, quizzes, midterm and final tests, and laboratory food order sheets already calculated and organized by food category for easy ordering and purchasing.

DONALD V. LACONI

Contents

1

Laboratory Conduct and Responsibilities

General Rules

1. Observe safety procedures while working with sharp knives and other equipment.
2. Keep your work station clean. Each student should assist in general housekeeping of the laboratory. You are responsible for washing your own equipment.
3. Be cooperative in sharing limited space and tools.
4. Inform the instructor of any physical disabilities that might cause danger to you or to another student while you work in the laboratory.
5. Never sit on any piece of equipment in the laboratory.
6. Return all equipment to its proper location in the laboratory. Each piece of equipment should be clean and dry before it is stored.

Personal Hygiene

1. Wash your hands with soap before working with food. Do not dry your hands on dish towels. Paper towels are available. Do not wear excessive jewelry.
2. After using a handkerchief, wash your hands before you handle food again.
3. Put on a chef hat before entering the laboratory, and do not remove it until after you leave the laboratory. Chef hats must be paper or linen only.
4. Avoid touching your hair or face while working with food. Wash your hands after each contact.
5. Use a special spoon or fork for sampling any food product to test for doneness or seasoning. Any spoon or fork placed in the mouth must be washed before being used for further food sampling.

Recommended Dress

Appropriate clothing for the food preparation laboratory includes the following items:

1. Clean white chef's jacket
2. Black-and-white checkered chef's pants
3. Clean white bib apron
4. Paper or linen chef hat
5. Black or white leather shoes
6. Name tag

Basic Tools

The following is essential equipment for your laboratory experience:

French knife   Liquid measuring cups
Boning knife   Ruler

Paring knife   Scissors

Potato peeler   Pencil and paper

Measuring spoons   Calculator

Dry measuring cups   Your text

A large tackle box works well to store your equipment. Remember that knives are viewed as weapons and must be carried in a secure manner. Make sure that each piece of your equipment has your name identification somewhere.

2

Sanitation and Safety

Good food is safe food. The foodservice manager's primary responsibility is to make certain that all employees are serving **safe** food to the public. Managers should obtain copies of all federal, state, and local sanitary codes and enforce these regulations strictly.

Food-Borne Diseases

Foodservice managers can eliminate and control food-borne diseases by using these practices:
▼ "Building in" sanitation in equipment
▼ Having proper storage facilities and refrigeration
▼ Employing and training healthy and careful workers
▼ Maintaining proper temperature controls with hot foods held over 140°F and cold foods under 40°F (See Figs. 2-1 and 2-2.)

Cooking alone will not guarantee the destruction of all food-borne bacteria, so it is necessary to start with safe food and handle it carefully.

Following are common food-borne diseases:

Botulism. Poisoning by a deadly toxin that results from improper processing or canning.

Trichinosis. A disease caused by larvae that are present in animal tissue—most often in pork. It is therefore necessary to cook all pork products thoroughly, to at least 150°F.

Typhoid fever. A disease caused by ingestion of contaminated milk or water or exposure to typhoid carriers.

Salmonellosis. A gastrointestinal infection caused by bacteria found in many animal products such as eggs, meats, dried yeasts, and fish. Growth of these bacteria can be prevented by **thorough cooking** and **proper refrigeration. Note:** Some salmonella organisms may survive freezing and may even multiply if frozen foods are not properly handled.

Staphylococcal poisoning. Poisoning caused by bacterial toxins growing in food. These can come from wounds or lesions on workers; thus it is absolutely essential to have a healthy, well-trained crew. Staphylococcal bacteria are resistant to heat, so thorough cooking is necessary to destroy them. Hold foods below 40°F and over 140°F.

Clostridium perfringens **poisoning.** A poisoning from various fungi and molds that are present in all environments. To control their growth, prevent their germination and multiplication by **preventing exposure to air** and **holding foods at proper temperatures** (cold foods under 40°F, hot foods over 140°F).

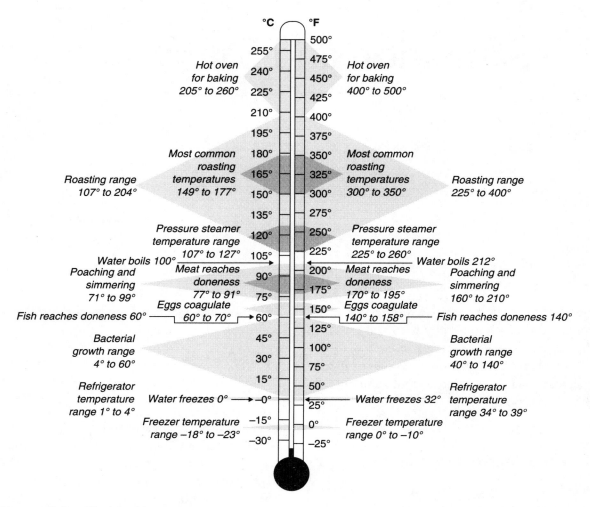

FIGURE 2-1   Kitchen Temperatures

Chemical poisoning. Caused by accidental ingestion of, or exposure to, cleaning products and the like. Take these steps to prevent it:

▼   Store all cleaning supplies, detergents, and insect and rodent poisons away from foods—preferably in a separate storage area.

▼   Label these products properly.

▼   Train all workers to read labels and to be sure of correct product to avoid mistakes.

▼   Keep MSDSs (material safety data sheets) accessible at all times.

Sanitation Rules

1. Get food hot as quickly as possible and keep it hot—140°F or over.

2. Get food cold as quickly as possible and keep it cold—40°F or below.

3. Keep food covered as much as possible; use clean utensils.

4. Exercise extreme caution when using leftovers. Do not prepare too much food ahead.

5. Wash all fresh fruits and vegetables.

6. Do not expose food to the danger temperature range (40°F to 140°F) for more than 3 hours.

7. Do not refreeze thawed meat, fish, or vegetables. Freezing and refreezing causes cellular breakdown and increases susceptibility to decay.

8. Make sure bent cans have not been punctured.

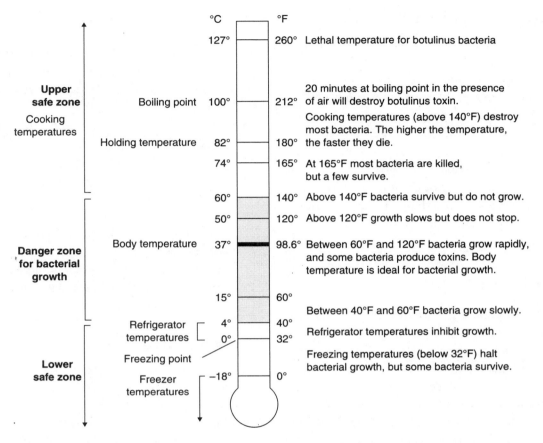

°C   °F

127°   260°   Lethal temperature for botulinus bacteria

Upper
safe zone   20 minutes at boiling point in the presence
                    Boiling point   100°   212°   of air will destroy botulinus toxin.
Cooking
temperatures   Cooking temperatures (above 140°F) destroy
                    Holding temperature 82° 180° most bacteria. The higher the temperature,
                                                   the faster they die.

                                    74°   165°   At 165°F most bacteria are killed,
                                                   but a few survive.

                                    60°   140°   Above 140°F bacteria survive but do not grow.

                                    50°   120°   Above 120°F growth slows but does not stop.

Danger zone   Body temperature 37°   98.6° Between 60°F and 120°F bacteria grow rapidly,
for bacterial   and some bacteria produce toxins. Body
growth   temperature is ideal for bacterial growth.

                                    15°   60°
                                                   Between 40°F and 60°F bacteria grow slowly.

                    Refrigerator   4°   40°   Refrigerator temperatures inhibit growth.
                    temperatures   0°   32°
                                                   Freezing temperatures (below 32°F) halt
                    Freezing point   bacterial growth, but some bacteria survive.
Lower
safe zone   Freezer   −18°   0°
                    temperatures

FIGURE 2-2   Temperature Safe Zones

9. Check all fish and shellfish for freshness when it is delivered to the property. Fresh fish have firm flesh, bright red gills, and clear eyes.
10. Cook all pork thoroughly.
11. Dispose of all garbage and rubbish promptly.
12. If in doubt about any food, throw it away.
13. Always sanitize your work area before beginning food production. Use a solution of bleach and water.

Dishwashing

Detailed instructions for dishwashing will be given at the laboratory orientation; here is a review of the important procedures. For reasons of sanitation and efficiency, dishwashing requires adequate equipment (preferably a dishwashing machine), adequate space, and a good source of water with proper temperature control.

Machine Dishwashing

1. Remove all food particles from dishes, using either a scraper or the rinse water power arm.
2. Pre-rinse dishes at 80°F. Wash at 140°F and rinse at 180°F. Avoid toweling dishes.
3. Store dishes in a clean, dry, enclosed storage area. Invert cups and glasses.
4. Any soap or detergent recommended by your supplier is adequate.

Hand Dishwashing

1. Use a sink with three compartments—one for washing, a second for rinsing in clean hot water, and a third for sanitizing dishes in some type of sanitizing agent.
2. Avoid towel drying your dishes.
3. Any soap or detergent recommended by your supplier is adequate.

Safe Pot and Pan Washing

1. Use a three-compartment sink or a pot-washing machine.
2. Scrape loosened food from dishes, pots, and flatware, then soak in warm water.
3. Wash in clean, soapy hot water. Use a pot-washing brush, and change water frequently. A detergent may be employed instead of soap.
4. Rinse in clean, hot chlorine solution (sanitizing agent) and drain. Toweling is not necessary if the rinse water is very hot.

Kitchen Safety

Safety and sanitation are directly related to each other; sometimes it's hard to separate them. The foodservice manager is responsible for establishing and maintaining safety standards, but the foodservice employees have an equal stake in preventing accidents and injuries. In Ohio alone, more than two thousand foodservice workers and managers are hurt on the job every year.

As you might expect, most accidents happen because of simple carelessness. Workers are in too much of a hurry—they don't pay attention to what they are doing, or they don't bother to read and follow safety procedures. It is a manager's responsibility to teach and demonstrate good safety practices, and then monitor employees with enthusiasm. Additionally, the Occupational Safety and Health Act (OSHA) requires that any foodservice establishment have a complete first aid kit available to employees at all times.

Slips and Falls

One-fourth of all accidents in the kitchen are slips and falls. Here are ways to prevent such accidents:

▼ Clean slippery materials from stairs and floors.
▼ Use wooden duck board or nonabrasive strips on hard-surfaced floors.
▼ Use abrasive covering in wet or greasy areas.
▼ Wipe up all liquid, food, or grease spills immediately.
▼ Keep all items off the floor. Do not store items on the floor even for a short time.
▼ Require employees to wear proper footwear.
▼ Discourage employees from running, walking quickly, or engaging in horseplay.
▼ Provide handrails in stairways.
▼ Provide adequate lighting in all work areas and stairwells.
▼ Do not overload serving trays. When loading a tray, be sure the server can see over and around it.
▼ Watch possible problem spots such as the floor around ice machines, deep fat fryers, and salad preparation areas.

Cuts and Bruises

Cuts and bruises are another common problem for foodservice workers. Help to prevent cuts and bruises by taking these measures:

▼ Post operation regulations for all equipment. Require strict observance of the regulations.
▼ Keep knives sharp, and use the proper knife for each job. Dull knives require more pressure than sharp ones and cause more cuts.
▼ Handle and clean knives properly. Clean with the cutting edge away from you. Use a paper towel or cloth towel. **Never wipe a knife on your apron.** If a knife or other implement falls, step back and allow it to hit the floor. Only a professional juggler can catch an airborne knife without grabbing the blade. Do not place knives or cutting blades from equipment in water-filled sinks. Wash these items immediately and put them away.
▼ Use a cutting board surface for cutting. Hold the food to be cut in a way that will prevent injury to your fingers. Slice a portion from the bottom of an unstable item to make a flatter surface and give you a better hold during the cutting process.
▼ Provide side towels so workers can keep their hands and utensils free from grease.

▼ Cut away from the body when using cutting tools.

▼ Use tampers to push food into choppers and grinding machines. Always use guards on power-driven machines.

▼ Sweep up broken glass or other sharp objects before washing the floors.

Burns

Burns present a serious and constant hazard to foodservice workers in every type of kitchen. They are a built-in danger, much like a microwave with a bad seal. But burns are avoidable. Follow these procedures to protect yourself and your crew:

▼ Require preparation employees to wear well-fitting uniforms with long sleeves. Expose as little skin as possible.

▼ Keep pot holders dry and readily available.

▼ Position equipment correctly. Remember that **all** equipment is potentially dangerous.

▼ Keep handles of pots and pans turned in from the edge of the stove, so that they cannot be knocked off and spill their contents.

▼ Never overfill a container with hot food. Allow enough freeboard to prevent splash and spillage.

▼ Water causes hot grease to "pop." Items to be deep-fried must be thoroughly drained and free of excess water. Be particularly careful with potatoes.

▼ In case of a minor burn or scald, put the injured part under cold water or apply ice immediately to prevent blistering and relieve pain.

Strains

Strains, like burns, are an almost constant hazard in the foodservice industry. And, like burns, they are preventable if you use a little common sense:

▼ When lifting, be sure your footing is secure.

▼ Get a firm grip on the item to be lifted.

▼ Lift with the heavy muscles of the legs so that the back is not strained. Bend knees and push while lifting.

▼ Do not obstruct your vision by stacking items too high.

▼ Arrange equipment properly so that extremely heavy loads do not have to be lifted.

▼ Set per-person weight limits, and require workers to ask for help when these limits are exceeded.

Mise en Place Sheet

Recipe title _____ **Yield** _____

Ingredients needed:

_____

_____

_____

_____

_____

_____

Equipment needed:

_____

_____

_____

_____

_____

_____

Procedure:

_____

_____

_____

_____

_____

_____

_____

_____

_____

_____

3

The Food Preparation Process

The Mise en Place

Every good chef knows that "mise en place" is the first step to successful food preparation. It means "putting in place." Organize the job beforehand: Get all needed materials together, and then keep things cleaned up and in order as you move toward the final goal during production.

All materials to be used, including small tools and hand equipment, should be within reach. Remember that knives need to be sharp, and **all** tools should be sanitized and in proper working order. Additionally, recipe items that need no cooking—such as chopped onions or carrots and grated cheese—should be ready and easily accessible.

From a manager's point of view, the use of a mise en place sheet like the one shown in Figure 3-1 will increase productivity and spare unnecessary work and movement. The mise en place is considered to be a motion economy technique.

Photocopy the mise en place sheet and use it for every recipe prepared in the laboratory.

Cutting Techniques

The most basic skill a cook must have is the ability to handle a knife quickly and efficiently to produce the exact size and shape of product needed. Although cutting machines often save time and labor, no machine can duplicate the versatility and judgment of an experienced cook with a good knife. The most basic cutting tool is the French knife, pictured in Figure 3-2. The following are some basic cutting techniques:

Cut. To divide into pieces or to shape using a knife.

Chop. To cut into pieces of no specified shape.

Mince. To chop very fine.

Dice. To cut into small, uniform cubes.

Slice. To cut into uniform slices, usually across the grain.

FIGURE 3-1   The Mise en Place Sheet

The French Knife

The French knife is a fairly thick, wide-bladed knife with a distinctive triangular shape. This knife is designed for heavy-duty cutting and chopping. Its sturdy blade is strong enough to withstand constant beating against the cutting board. The blade extends well below the knife handle, allowing the fingers to encircle the handle without hitting the board.

The French knife is used for many operations, such as cutting, mincing, and pureeing. A cook needs much practice to master these operations with speed and accuracy. Your instructor will demonstrate correct techniques for using a French knife, then will supervise you as you try it yourself.

For a comfortable position while working, first stand at arm's length from the work surface with your heels together at a 45° angle. Then take a short step forward—with your left foot if you are right-handed, with your right foot if you are left-handed. Your body is now at a 45° angle to the cutting board. This position allows natural movement of your shoulder, arm, and hand, all in line with one another. It will reduce

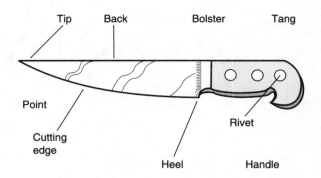

FIGURE 3-2   The French Knife

fatigue, especially when you are working for long periods.

Begin by holding the knife correctly. Hold the base of the blade with your thumb and forefinger. Relax the remaining fingers loosely around the handle. This gives you good control. Many beginners hold the knife far back on the handle and push down with a forefinger along the top of the blade. The correct grip takes less effort and gives far more control because the knife is in balance. A simple wrist motion makes the weight of the knife itself do a good bit of the work.

CUTTING EQUIPMENT TERMS

Boning knife: A tool for cutting around bone and gristle

Bread knife: A serrated slicing tool for cutting breads

Butcher's knife: A tool for cutting meats into individual servings

Chef's knife: A basic tool for cutting, chopping, or dicing vegetables

Cleaver: A tool for cutting through bones and for chopping or slicing vegetables

Ham slicer: A tool for making long, even slices of ham

Knife: A tool for cutting, slicing, chopping, or grating food

Meat fork: A two-pronged fork inserted into

meat to hold it while it is being sliced or moved to a serving platter

Paring knife: A smaller chef's tool for peeling, slicing, or cutting

Peeler: A tool for removing vegetable skins

Scimitar knife: A special tool with a turned-up blade tip for cutting portions of meat

Sharpening steel: A long steel rod for raising the edges of a knife

Sharpening stone: A stone for grinding the cutting edge of a knife

Skinning knife: A tool for cutting between fatty tissue and the meat itself

Slicing knife: A tool for slicing through meats or breads

Utility knife: A tool for many different functions

Other Equipment

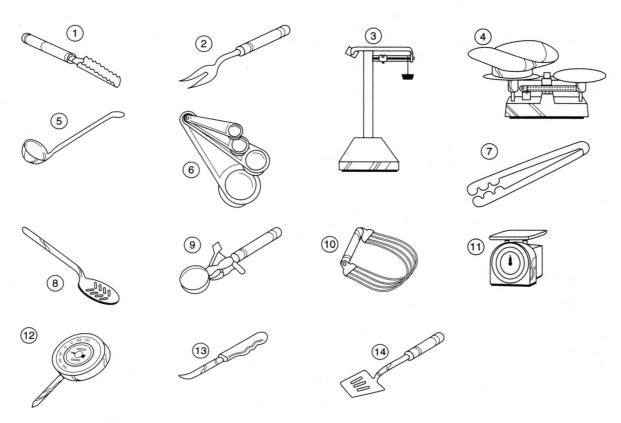

FIGURE 3-3   Knives, Tools, and Measuring Devices: (1) apple corer, (2) two-tine fork, (3) large balance scale, (4) small balance scale, (5) ladle, (6) measuring spoons, (7) tongs, (8) slotted spoon, (9) ice-cream scoop, (10) pastry blender, (11) spring scale, (12) meat thermometer, (13) citrus knife, (14) turner

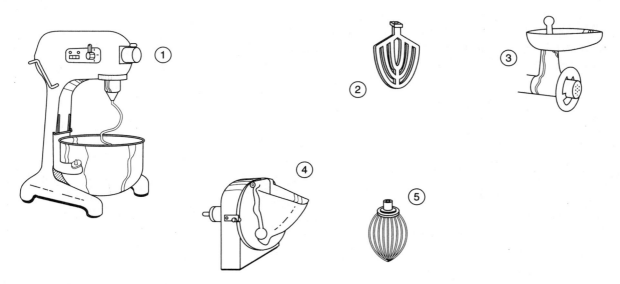

FIGURE 3-4   Mixer Attachments: (1) dough hook, (2) paddle, (3) food grinder, (4) food grater, (5) whip

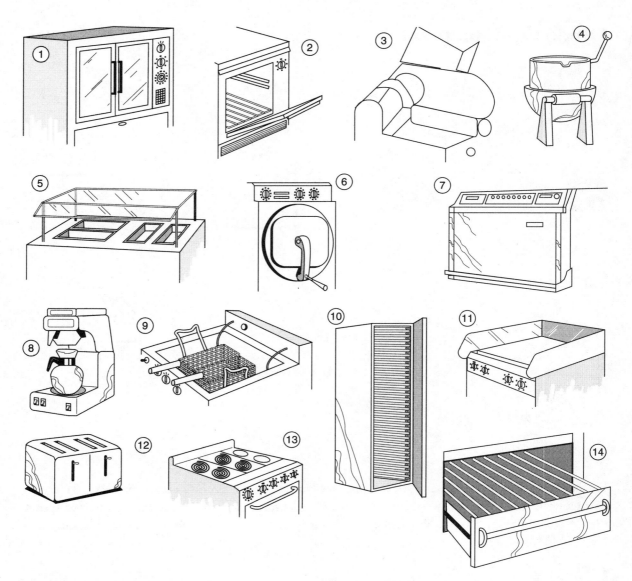

FIGURE 3-5   Cooking Equipment: (1) convection oven, (2) conventional oven, (3) meat slicer, (4) steam-jacketed kettle, (5) steam table, (6) pressure cooker, (7) microwave oven, (8) coffee-maker, (9) deep-fat fryer, (10) proof box, (11) griddle/grill, (12) toaster, (13) stovetop, (14) broiler

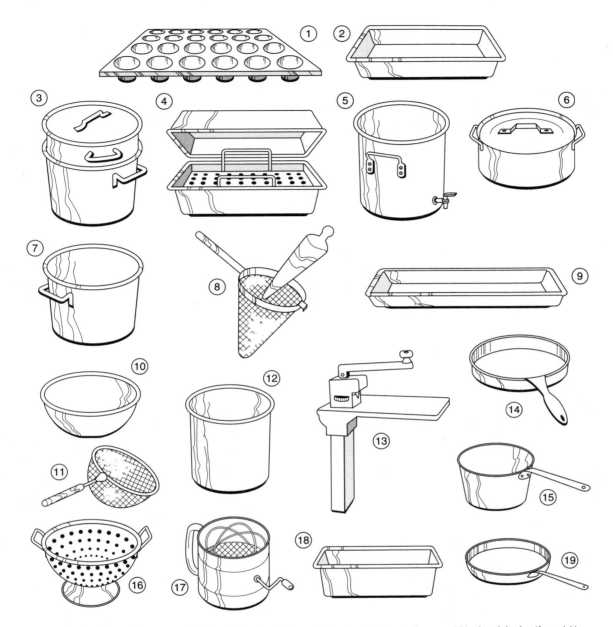

FIGURE 3-6   Pots, Pans, and Other Tools: (1) muffin tin, (2) hotel pan, (3) double boiler, (4) roasting pan, (5) stockpot, (6) braiser, (7) saucepot, (8) China cap, (9) sheet pan, (10) mixing bowl, (11) strainer, (12) bain-marie, (13) can opener, (14) iron skillet, (15) saucepan, (16) colander, (17) flour sifter, (18) bread pan, (19) sauté pan

4

The Cooking Process

Transfer of Heat

Conduction

Conduction is the movement of heat through a solid material. The heat moves from one molecule of matter to the next, and eventually spreads through the whole substance. For example, the electrical element embedded in an iron griddle becomes hot. Because the element is touching the iron, the heat flows from it throughout the griddle. In cooking, heat is transferred through the burner, into the pot, into the water or fat, and finally into the food.

There are several conducting media. Copper and aluminum are very good conductors of heat. Iron is not a bad conductor. Stainless steel is a very poor conductor. (Stainless steel frying pans and other equipment usually have copper-clad bottoms so the copper can pick up the heat and transfer it evenly into the pan.)

Convection

Convection is the movement of heat in liquid or gas. Hot air rises because it expands, becoming lighter than cold air. The cold air then descends to become heated. As the cold air is heated, it rises. At the same time, the air that previously rose has cooled and now descends. Thus we have a circular motion of air picking up heat, carrying it away, and then returning to get more heat again.

In a convection oven, heat is moved by a fan that moves or convects the hot air throughout the oven. A convection oven is more efficient than a regular oven, which depends upon natural convection. Natural convection does not distribute the heat as well.

Convection is also possible with hot liquids like water or fat and with certain gases. A refrigerator, for instance, works because a liquid—the refrigerant—picks up heat and moves it away.

Radiation

Radiation is the transfer of heat by wave energy. Radiated heat moves about 186,000 miles per second. Broilers and toasters cook largely by radiation. Tiny particles of energy flow from a hot body to a cooler one.

White heat emits the most radiation. Red glowing heat gives off some radiation in the infrared wave range, but an object glowing with white heat will give off more radiant energy. Thus some broilers have ceramic particles that heat to white heat.

A dark object will absorb heat more readily than a lighter one. Aluminum pans containing frozen foods should be black on the outside because a shiny object reflects radiated heat away. (That's why many ovens have heat deflectors.) A bright aluminum pan will not bake a pie as nicely as a duller one. When wrapping food to hold the heat in, put the shiny aluminum side inside so it bounces the heat back. To keep heat from getting in, put the shiny aluminum side on the outside.

Moist Heat Cooking Methods

Boiling, Simmering, Poaching, and Blanching

The terms **boil, simmer,** and **poach** all mean to cook a food in water or in a seasoned and flavored liquid. The temperature of the liquid determines the method. When a food is to be simmered or boiled, bring the liquid to a full boil at first. (This compensates for the lowering of the temperature when the food items are added.) Then adjust the heat to maintain a steady temperature.

To **boil** means to cook in a liquid that is bubbling rapidly and is greatly agitated. Water boils at 212°F. No matter how high the burner is turned, the temperature of the liquid will go no higher. (It is possible to heat steam to much higher temperatures, but that will be discussed later.) Boiling is generally reserved for certain vegetables and starches. High temperatures tend to toughen the proteins in meats, fish, and eggs, and rapid bubbling usually breaks up delicate foods.

To **simmer** means to cook in a liquid that is bubbling very gently. The temperature is about 185° to 205°F. Most foods cooked in liquid are simmered. The higher temperatures and intense agitation of boiling are detrimental to most foods. The word *boiled* is sometimes used as a menu term, as when simmered fresh beef is called "boiled beef."

To **poach** means to cook in a small amount of liquid that is hot but not actually bubbling. The temperature is about 160° to 180°F. Poaching is used to cook delicate foods such as fish and eggs out of the shell. It is also used to partially cook foods such as varietal meats, to eliminate undesirable flavors, and to firm up the product before final cooking.

To **blanch** means to cook an item partially and very briefly, usually in water but sometimes by other methods. There are two ways of blanching in water:

1. Place the item in cold water, bring to a boil, and simmer briefly. Cool the item by plunging it into cold water. The purpose is to dissolve blood, salt, or impurities from certain meats and bones.
2. Place the item in rapidly boiling water and return the water to a boil. Remove the item and cool in cold water. The purpose is to set the color and destroy harmful enzymes in vegetables or to loosen the skins of tomatoes, peaches, and similar items for easier peeling.

Steaming

To **steam** means to cook foods by exposing them directly to steam. For large quantities of food this is usually done in steam cookers specially designed to accept standard-sized pans. Food can also be steamed on a rack above boiling water. This method is cumbersome, however, and is not often used in food service. Steaming also refers to cooking an item tightly wrapped or covered so that it cooks in the steam formed by its own moisture. Cooking in a steam-jacketed kettle is not steaming because the steam does not actually touch the food.

Widely used for vegetables, steaming cooks them rapidly, without agitation, and minimizes the loss of nutrients that usually occurs when vegetables are cooked.

Steam at normal pressure is 212°F—the same as boiling water. However, because steam carries much more heat than boiling water and cooks very rapidly, you must carefully control cooking times to avoid overcooking.

A pressure steamer is a cooker that holds in steam under pressure. The temperature of the steam then goes higher than 212°F. Because of the elevated temperatures, pressure steaming is an extremely rapid method of cooking and must be very carefully controlled and timed.

Braising

To **braise** means to cook covered in a small amount of liquid, usually after browning. Braised meats are usually browned first, with a dry heat method such as panfrying. Browning gives a desirable appearance and flavor to the meat and the sauce. Some vegetables, such as lettuce, or cabbage, are very flavorful when braised at a low temperature in a small amount of liquid.

In braising, the food is usually not completely covered by the cooking liquid. The top of the product is actually cooked by the steam held in the covered pot. A pot roast, for example, is cooked in liquid covering only one-third to two-thirds of the meat. This method yields a flavorful, concentrated sauce. The exact amount of cooking liquid depends on how much sauce is needed.

In some preparations, especially of poultry and fish, no liquid is added. This is still considered braising because steam is trapped by the cover and the item cooks in its own moisture.

Braising may be done on the range or in the oven. Braising in the oven has three major advantages:

1. The food cooks uniformly. The heat strikes the braising pot on all sides, not just on the bottom.
2. Less attention is required. Foods braise at a low, steady temperature without having to be checked constantly.
3. Range space is free for other purposes.

Dry Heat Cooking Methods

Roasting and Baking

To **roast** and to **bake** mean to cook foods by surrounding them with hot, dry air, usually in an oven. Cooking on a spit over an open fire is also roasting.

▼ **Roasting** usually applies to meats and poultry.

▼ **Baking** applies to breads, pastries, vegetables, and fish. It is a more general term than roasting.

Cooking uncovered is essential to roasting. Covering holds in steam, changing the process from dry heat to moist heat cooking, such as braising or steaming.

Meat is roasted on a rack. The rack prevents the meat from simmering in its own juices and fat. It also allows hot air to circulate all around the meat. When roasting in a conventional oven, allow for uneven temperatures by changing the position of the meat occasionally. The back of the oven is usually hotter because heat is lost at the door.

Broiling

To **broil** means to cook with radiant heat from above. Broiling is a fast, high-heat method usually used for tender meats, poultry, fish, and a few vegetable items. A low-intensity broiler called a **salamander** is used for browning or melting the tops of some items before service.

Note the following rules for broiling:

▼ Turn heat on full. Regulate the cooking temperature by moving the rack nearer to or farther from the heat.

▼ Use lower heat for larger, thicker cuts and for items to be cooked well done. Use higher heat for thinner pieces and for items to be cooked rare. This is necessary so that the inside and outside are done at the same time. It takes a lot of practice and experience to cook foods of different thicknesses with the desired amount of surface browning **and** the right degree of doneness inside.

▼ Preheat the broiler. Preheating helps sear the meat quickly, and a hot broiler makes the desired grill marks on the food.

▼ Dip foods in oil to prevent sticking and to minimize drying. **Warning: Too much oil on a hot broiler grate may cause a fire.**

▼ Avoid unnecessary handling. Turn foods over only once, to cook on both sides.

Grilling, Griddling, and Pan Broiling

Grilling, griddling, and **pan broiling** are all dry heat cooking methods that use heat from below. **Grilling** is done on an open grid over charcoal, an electric element, or a gas-heated elements. Regulate the cooking temperature by moving the foods to hotter or cooler places on the grill. Turn grilled meats to achieve desired marking, as in broiling.

Griddling is done on a solid cooking surface, with or without small amounts of fat to prevent sticking. The temperature is adjustable and is much lower than on a grill. In addition to meats, items such as eggs and pancakes are cooked on a griddle.

Pan broiling is like griddling, except that it is done in a sauté pan or skillet instead of on a griddle surface. Fat must be poured off as it accumulates, or the process becomes panfrying. To prevent steaming, add no liquid, and do not cover the pan.

Frying

Panfrying and Sautéing

To **panfry** means to cook in a moderate amount of fat in a pan over moderate heat. Although more fat is used, panfrying is similar to sautéing. This method is used for larger pieces of food, such as chops and chicken pieces, and the items are not tossed by a flip of the pan as they are in sautéing. The amount of fat used depends on the food being cooked. Only a small amount of fat is used for eggs, for example, while as much as an inch or more may be used for panfried chicken.

Panfrying is usually done over lower heat than sautéing because larger pieces are being cooked. The lower temperature usually makes cooking time longer. Although most foods must be turned at least once for even cooking, some larger foods must be removed from the pan and finished in the oven so excessive surface browning will be prevented.

To **sauté** means to cook quickly in a small amount of fat. There are two important principles to sautéing:

1. Preheat the pan before adding the food to be sautéed. The food must be seared quickly or it will begin to simmer in its own juices.

2. Do not overcrowd the pan. Overcrowding lowers the temperature too much, and again the food is not seared but begins to simmer in its own juices.

Meats to be sautéed are often dusted with flour; this prevents sticking and helps achieve uniform browning. After food is sautéed, a liquid such as wine or stock is often swirled in the pan to dissolve browned bits of food sticking to the bottom. This is called **deglazing.** This liquid becomes part of the sauce served with sautéed items.

Deep-Frying

To **deep-fry** means to cook submerged in hot fat. A quality deep-fried food is characterized by the following properties:
▼ A minimum of liquid fat absorption
▼ Very little moisture loss
▼ An attractive golden color
▼ A crisp surface or coating
▼ No "off" flavors from the frying fat

Many foods are dipped in a breading or batter before frying. This forms a protective coating between the food and the fat (to help prevent absorption) and adds crispness, color, and flavor. Obviously, the quality of the breading or batter affects the quality of the finished product.

Microwave Cooking

Microwave cooking refers to the use of a specific tool rather than to a cooking method. Both dry and moist heat may be employed with the microwave oven. This piece of equipment is used mostly for heating prepared foods and for thawing. However, it can be used for primary cooking as well.

The microwave oven is a unique tool in food service. The cook should observe the following special points regarding its use:
▼ Small items will not brown in a standard microwave. Large roasts may brown a little from the heat generated within the meat

itself. Some microwave ovens have added browning elements that use conventional heat.

▼ Overcooking is the most common error in microwave use, so watch timing carefully. High energy levels cook small items very rapidly.

▼ Large items should be turned once or twice for even cooking.

▼ An on-off cycle is often used for large items, to allow time for heat to be conducted to the interior.

▼ No metal may be used in a microwave oven because it would shield foods from the radiant energy. Furthermore, the reflected microwaves could damage the magnetron, which is the machine's generator.

▼ Because microwaves cook so rapidly, they will not break down the connective tissues of less tender cuts of meats. Slow, moist cooking is necessary.

▼ The more food is placed in the microwave at one time, the longer it takes to cook. Thus the primary advantage of microwave cooking—speed—is lost with large roasts.

5

Standardized Recipes and Measurement

Each foodservice unit should establish its own file of standard recipes. Selected recipes may be kept in books, on separate sheets, or on cards. After recipes are tested and standardized, create an index (preferably a computer index) to permit more flexibility in filing. The system should usually follow your menu pattern, and the recipes should be kept in an area of easy access.

Before writing recipes, standardize the following operations and equipment:

▼ Equipment needed and techniques for weighing
▼ Sizes of pans in relation to yields
▼ Yields or serving sizes
▼ Serving equipment
▼ Ingredients
▼ Methods and techniques for mixing

Advantages of Standardizing

1. It saves time for both the cook and the manager, allowing more time for skill and consistency in preparing, serving, and merchandising foods.
2. It eliminates guesswork and waste due to inaccurate estimates of quantity and errors in cooking.

3. It eliminates variations in the quality and quantity of foods and makes frequent sampling and "doctoring" unnecessary.
4. It simplifies the training of new workers.
5. It assists in food cost control by providing a means of
   — Figuring accurate costs of ingredients used
   — Estimating the expected yield more accurately
   — Curbing losses and preventing unnecessary adjustments by use of fewer or cheaper ingredients
   — Maintaining quality
   — Minimizing leftovers

Setting Up a Standardized Recipe

1. Choose the most practical form to use.
2. Determine the desired yield of the recipe.
3. Decide whether to use weights, measures, or both. The usual procedure is to use measures for liquids and for dry ingredients in quantities under 25 servings and to weigh larger quantities of dry ingredients.
4. Use the same abbreviations in all recipes (see Fig. 5-1). Be sure the abbreviations are easy to read.

UNIT OF MEASURE	ABBREVIATION
Teaspoon	tsp or t
Tablespoon	Tb, Tbsp, tbsp, or T
Cup	C, c, or Cp
Fluid ounce	fl oz
Pint	pt
Quart	qt
Gallon	gal or g
Ounce	oz
Pound	lb or #

FIGURE 5-1   Abbreviations for Units of Measure

5. Express all quantities in usable figures. Avoid fractions. Convert all measures into the largest possible unit. (See Fig. 5-2 for equivalencies among units of measure.)

6. List all ingredients in the order used, and use correct terminology and any necessary qualifying statements.

7. Give directions in detailed, concise, and exact terms.

8. Include serving directions.

9. Calculate and state the cost of the recipe. Check for seasonal changes in cost that might affect the selling price.

10. Retest and revise all recipes occasionally for . . .
    — Accuracy
    — Improved and new methods
    — Time-saving steps

11. Upgrade your file frequently with new ideas from pictures, clippings, and your own dining-out experiences. Notice variations in garnishes or food combinations.

Measuring Devices

Here are the measuring devices that you will use in following standardized recipes:

Scales. Used for measuring ingredients as well as for portioning products for service. Most recipe ingredients are measured by weight, so accurate scales are very important.

Volume measures. Used for liquids. Volume measures have lips for easy pouring. Sizes are pint, quart, half gallon, and gallon. Each size is marked off into fourths by ridges on the sides.

Measuring cups. Used for both liquid and dry measures. Measuring cups are available in 1-cup, ½-cup, ⅓-cup, and ¼-cup sizes.

Measuring spoons. Used for measuring very small volumes: 1 tablespoon, 1 teaspoon, ½ teaspoon, and ¼ teaspoon. They are used most often for spices and seasonings.

Ladles. Used for measuring and portioning liquids. The size of a ladle, in ounces, is stamped on the handle.

Scoops. Used for portioning soft solid foods. Scoops come in standard sizes and have levers

	tsp	tbsp	fl oz	c	pt	qt	gal
1 tsp	1	⅓	⅙	¹⁄₄₈	¹⁄₉₆	¹⁄₁₉₂	¹⁄₇₆₈
1 tbsp	3	1	½	¹⁄₁₆	¹⁄₃₂	¹⁄₆₄	¹⁄₂₅₆
1 fl oz	6	2	1	⅛	¹⁄₁₆	¹⁄₃₂	¹⁄₁₂₈
1 c	48	16	8	1	½	¼	¹⁄₁₆
1 pt	96	32	16	2	1	½	⅛
1 qt	192	64	32	4	2	1	¼
1 gal	768	256	128	16	8	4	1

FIGURE 5-2   Equivalents

for mechanical release. Scoop sizes are listed in Figure 5-3. The number of the scoop indicates the number of level scoops per quart. In actual use, a rounded scoopful is often more practical, so the exact weight will vary.

SCOOP NUMBER	VOLUME	APPROXIMATE WEIGHT
6	⅔ c	5 oz
8	½ c	4 oz
10	3 fl oz	3–3½ oz
12	⅓ c	2½–3 oz
16	¼ c	2–2½ oz
20	1½ fl oz	1¾ oz
24	1⅓ fl oz	1⅓ oz
30	1 fl oz	1 oz
40	0.8 fl oz	0.8 oz
60	½ fl oz	½ oz

FIGURE 5-3   Scoop Sizes

Enlarging Recipes

Here are the procedures for enlarging recipes. When expanding a recipe, keep in mind that the product may change because of chemical changes or reactions.

1. Evaluate the small recipe as to proportions, method, cost, and yield. Decide whether it is correct, practical, and suitable for your use.
2. Have a tester or skilled worker double the recipe, and assign a panel to evaluate the results. Run several tests if necessary. **Document any change to the final product.**
3. Enlarge the recipe to 50 or 100 servings. Make any necessary modifications or adjustments for time, temperature, or method. Convert all amounts to weights when possible, and check your figures for accuracy and usability. Check instructions for clarity, conciseness, and accuracy. Make any necessary modifications. **Document any changes to the final product.**
4. Have a tester make the larger quantity, and evaluate those results. Several tests may be necessary.
5. Have the cook prepare the larger recipe, and test the quality.
6. Run a popularity, cost, and yield study.
7. Send the enlarged recipe out to other units if possible, and require a report of results.
8. If the final product is satisfactory, incorporate the newer, enlarged recipe in your file as a standardized recipe.

Eggs Benedict

Yield = 10 Portions		Yield = 48 Portions	
INGREDIENTS NEEDED	**EQUIPMENT NEEDED**	**INGREDIENTS NEEDED**	**EQUIPMENT NEEDED**
10 English muffins	*Liquid measures*	*4 dz English muffins*	*Liquid measures*
20 Eggs	*Metal spatula*	*8 dz Eggs*	*Metal spatula*
20 2-oz slices Canadian bacon	*1½ oz ladle*	*12 lb Canadian bacon cut in 2-oz slices*	*1½ oz ladle*
12½ oz Hollandaise sauce	*Sauté pan*	*2 qt Hollandaise sauce*	*Broiler*
			Meat slicer

Note that *Ingredients Needed* changed from individual to quantity measures and that *Equipment Needed* changed from a Sauté pan to a broiler and meat slicer.

7

Costing Recipes

When a recipe is standardized for use, the costs of all the ingredients that go into the recipe are totaled, and a per-unit cost is figured. For example, if the recipe yields 50 chicken pies, add up the costs of all the ingredients needed to make the 50 pies to get the cost of the recipe. Divide that total cost by 50 to find the unit cost (the cost of 1 chicken pie).

You must know the exact number of servings or yield. Knowing the exact per-unit cost of a food item helps the manager decide how much should be charged for it when it is served.

Prices of ingredients change from time to time, so it is necessary to refigure the unit cost periodically. If the costs change too much, it may be necessary to change the menu price.

The cost sheets of all food and beverage establishments will not look exactly alike, but they will be similar and will provide the same information—how much it costs *per unit* to produce a chicken pie, a turkey sandwich, a plate of spaghetti, or whatever the product. Figure 7-1 shows a typical cost sheet for a standard recipe for ragout of lamb. Figure 7-2 outlines the steps for costing a recipe.

Item:	Ragout of lamb
Yield:	13 portions
Size of portion:	4 oz meat; 9 oz total

INGREDIENT	QUANTITY (×)	MARKET PRICE (=)	EXTENSION (COST)
Lamb (¾)	6 lb	$2.90 per lb	$17.40
Roux: Butter	8 oz	.80 per lb	.40
Flour	8 oz	.085 per lb	.043
Lamb stock bones	1 lb 12 oz	No charge	—
Carrots	12 oz	.35 per lb	.226
Celery	12 oz	.28 per lb	.15
Onions	12 oz	.20 per lb	.15

Total cost: $18.429 ($18.429 ÷ 13) = **Cost per portion: $1.42**

FIGURE 7-1　Cost Sheet for a Ragout of Lamb

1. Find the as-purchased (AP) cost of each ingredient.
2. Convert the recipe amount of the ingredient and the AP amount to the same unit of measure. Usually you would convert the AP unit of measure (e.g., gallons, below) to the recipe unit of measure (e.g., pints). Occasionally you would do it the other way around (e.g., number of eggs to dozens).
3. Find the cost of 1 unit by dividing the AP cost by the number of units.
4. Find the recipe cost of the ingredient by multiplying the cost of 1 unit by the number of units the recipe calls for.
5. Find the total cost of the recipe by adding up all the ingredient costs.
6. Find the cost per portion by dividing the total recipe cost by the number of portions (yield).

FOR EXAMPLE:

THOUSAND ISLAND DRESSING

Yield: 1 qt (1 L) or 32 1-oz (30-g) portions

INGREDIENTS	STEP 1 AP COST	STEP 2 UNIT CONVERSION	STEP 3 UNIT COST	STEP 4 RECIPE COST
1½ pt mayonnaise	5.21 per gal	1 gal = 8 pt	$\frac{5.21}{8} = 0.651$	$0.651 \times 1.5 = 0.977$
¼ pt chili sauce	3.57 per #10 can	1 can = 6 pt	$\frac{3.57}{6} = 0.595$	$0.595 \times 0.25 = 0.149$
¼ pt catsup	3.29 per #10 can	1 can = 6 pt	$\frac{3.29}{6} = 0.548$	$0.548 \times 0.25 = 0.137$
6 eggs	0.91 per dozen	6 eggs = ½ dozen	0.91	$0.91 \times 0.5 = 0.455$
2 oz onions	0.11 per lb	1 lb = 16 oz	$\frac{0.11}{16} = 0.007$	$0.007 \times 2 = 0.014$
2 oz dill pickles	0.99 per lb	1 lb = 16 oz	$\frac{0.99}{16} = 0.062$	$0.062 \times 2 = 0.124$

Step 5: Total recipe cost: 1.856

Step 6: $\dfrac{\text{cost of recipe}}{\text{number of portions}} \quad \dfrac{1.856}{32} = 0.058$ Cost per portion

FIGURE 7-2   How to Cost a Recipe

8

Measuring Temperatures

Choosing the Right Food Thermometer

Various kinds of thermometers are used in the foodservice industry. Some are used to check temperatures of equipment and storage areas. Built-in or hang-type thermometers are usually required in refrigerator and freezer units. Thermometers are also built into hot-holding equipment and dishwashing machines. Others are used to check temperatures of food. Because temperature control is such an integral part of food sanitation, choosing the appropriate food thermometer and using it properly are of critical importance.

The most versatile type of thermometer for checking food temperature is the bimetallic thermometer. The thermometer must be numerically scaled, easily readable, and accurate. The metal stem should be at least 5 inches long, with the lower 2 inches being the sensing area for immersion into foods. A thermometer of this type usually has a calibration nut so that the user can adjust it to maintain maximum accuracy.

Thermometers with a scale ranging from 0°F to 220°F can be used to check the temperatures of incoming shipments of frozen and refrigerated food products; final cooking temperatures; food temperatures in coolers, freezers, and hot-holding units; and the temperatures of sanitizing solutions. A bimetallic thermometer with a plastic lens cover should not be left in food

during cooking. **A glass or mercury-filled thermometer should never be used to measure food temperatures.**

Using Food Thermometers

After selecting an appropriate thermometer, the sanitation-conscientious manager must be sure that each device is used properly and that it functions as an instrument of sanitation, not a contributor to contamination. Following a few simple rules will ensure this.

1. Sanitize the thermometer before each use to eliminate any contamination. A sanitizing solution appropriate to other food-contact surfaces may be used. Alcohol swabs are also recommended because they are inexpensive, portable, and readily available from medical supply houses.
2. Take the temperature in the thermal center of the food item. This is usually the center of the thickest part, although composition of the food being tested may alter the heat distribution. Allow 15 seconds after the indicator stops moving, then record the reading.
3. Recalibrate or adjust the accuracy of the thermometer periodically . . . especially

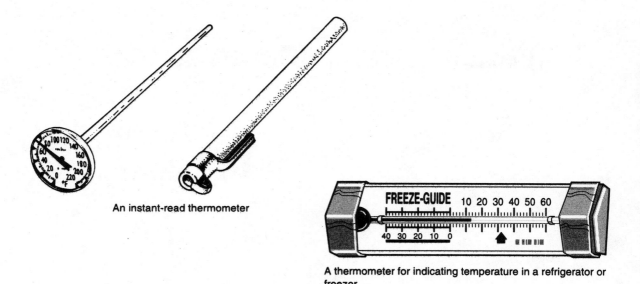

An instant-read thermometer

A thermometer for indicating temperature in a refrigerator or freezer

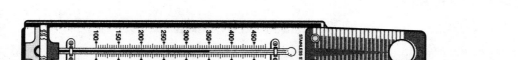

A thermometer for testing the temperature of the fat in the deep fryer

FIGURE 8-1   Types of Thermometers

after an extreme temperature change or if the thermometer has been dropped. You can do this by inserting the sensing area of the thermometer into an ice water slush until the indicator stabilizes, and then adjusting the calibration nut so the indicator reads 32°F.

Figure 8-1 shows various types of thermometers used in foodservice operations.

9

Stocks and Soups

Stocks are the bases of many soups and sauces that are prepared and handled in a similar manner. The difference between individual soups and sauces often is only a matter of consistency, seasoning, or slight variation in ingredients. **Soup** is a liquid food consisting mainly of the broth of meat, seafood, or vegetables.

Stocks

Stocks are thin, flavored liquids derived from meat, fish, or poultry bones simmered with vegetables and seasonings. Simmering extracts the flavors and results in a rich, flavorful stock. To make a good stock you need the right ingredients, preparation methods, and aftercare.

Ingredients

A quality stock results only when clean, wholesome ingredients in the right quantities are used. The right equipment also must be employed.

To make 1 gallon of stock, you need 4 pounds of bones, 5 quarts of cold water, 1 pound of mirepoix (50 percent onions or leeks, 25 percent carrots), and seasonings. The bones should be trimmed of meat for economic reasons and cut into 4-inch lengths or cracked to increase surface area. Small pieces of meat, fish, or poultry may be added to give flavor to the stock. A large piece of meat also could be simmered with the stock if it were needed later. The best beef bones to use are the knuckle, shank, and neck bones, in that order. An excellent stock can be made from a chicken carcass or chicken parts (back, wings, neck). The bones of lean white fish such as haddock, sole, and cod make a light, delicate stock.

Mirepoix is a mixture of roughly cut vegetables of high quality. Many mirepoix mixtures contain vegetables such as parsley, turnips, or cabbage, depending on the flavors desired. To enhance their stocks many cooks use various ingredients such as good trimmings of mushrooms or parsley and chicken or roast carcasses after they are trimmed of meat. However, the stockpot is not a garbage can in which to put all wastes regardless of quality or flavor.

Various seasonings such as bay leaves, thyme, cloves, peppercorns, garlic, and parsley stems also are added to the stock. These herbs and spices are usually wrapped in a small cloth or bag called a **sachet bag** or between two stalks of celery in a form called a **bouquet garni.** Add only enough salt to help make the products more soluble. Because stocks often are concentrated or combined with other foods, too much salt in the stock may oversalt the product.

The equipment needed for making stock is very simple. Bones should be cut and cracked in the meat processing area, which has a band saw, cleavers, and meat blocks. A stockpot can be used for range cooking; a steam-jacketed kettle also can be used. A good stockpot should have a spigot so the stock can be withdrawn from the bottom. A cutting board, a French knife for preparing vegetables, a ladle, a skimmer, and a china cap (a conical-shaped sieve) also are required.

Preparation Methods

A good meat stock can be extracted in 8 hours, although some meat stocks may be simmered for 12 to 24 hours. Fish stocks cannot be simmered more than 2 hours or chicken stocks more than 6 hours without clouding.

 Certain common procedures are essential to preparation of a good stock. Place the bones in a stockpot, add enough cold water to cover them, and bring the pot to a boil. From the top, skim off the scum (coagulated protein). Then lower the temperature to simmer.

 Most chefs start their stocks from cold water, saying that the stock has more flavor or that they get a clearer stock. The scum remains in the bones and does not become free in the stock.

 The mirepoix and seasonings may be included with the bones at the start or added later as the stock simmers, depending on the type of stock. When the stock is done, it is drawn through the spigot or poured from the pot into a china cap covered with cheesecloth. It can be used immediately or stored for later use.

Classification of Stocks

Stocks are classified according to ingredients and color. The four major types are: brown stock, white stock, chicken stock, and fish stock.

Brown Stock

Brown stock usually is made of beef and veal bones. Beef bones—from a more mature animal—give a rich flavor. Veal bones—from a younger animal—provide gelatin that gives body to the stock.

 Oil the bones lightly, place them in roasting pans, and brown in an oven until golden brown. Overbrowned bones produce a bitter stock; underbrowned bones yield a stock that is weak in flavor and poorly colored.

After browning the bones, put them into the stockpot. Pour the fat off the roasting pan bottom, and deglaze the pan by removing the browned portion with water over a hot surface. Add this liquid to the stockpot, and cover the bones with water. Bring to a boil, skim, and simmer for 6 to 8 hours. Add the mirepoix and sachet about midway in the cooking period. Some chefs add tomatoes to enrich the color and give more flavor.

White Stock

White stock is more delicately flavored than brown stock. Veal bones are ideal for white stock, but beef and veal bones may be used together. **The bones are not browned.** They are cut, washed, and placed in cold water, which is then brought to a boil. Change the water if the stock appears cloudy at the start. Simmer from 4 to 6 hours. Add the mirepoix and sachet about halfway through. The finished stock is strained and used or stored.

Chicken Stock

Chicken stock also can be called a white stock. It is prepared in the same way as white stock but is simmered for only 2 to 3 hours. Add the mirepoix and seasonings after the first hour of simmering. For white stocks some chefs eliminate the carrots from the mirepoix to assure proper coloring, but this is a matter of personal preference. Chicken stock must always be strained before use or storage.

Fish Stock

Bones, heads, skins, and trimmings from white, lean, deep-sea fish are typically used for a **fish stock.** Rich, fatty fish such as salmon, mackerel, or trout give a strong and slightly dark stock. Do not wash the fish bones; because the cooking time is so short, the delicate flavor may be washed away. Cold water containing the bones and trimmings is brought to a boil, skimmed, and simmered. Add the mirepoix and seasonings immediately after skimming.

 An acid such as lemon juice often is added to the simmering fish stock. Simmer only 30 to

45 minutes. Overcooking will cause the stock to become cloudy.

Glaze, Essence, and Fumet

A **glaze** is a stock that has been strained and simmered until reduced one-fourth in volume. The mixture is syrupy and will coat a spoon. A stock simmered until half the volume is lost is called a **demi-glaze.** Glazes and demi-glazes are used to enhance the flavor of soups and sauces or to enrich the final product.

An **essence** also is a rich stock. It is used to flavor and enrich items. It contains a rich stock, wine, vegetables, and herbs. After simmering, the liquid is strained and reduced to the desired consistency—usually that of a demi-glaze. Some popular essences are ham, fish, mushroom, chicken, and game.

A **fumet** is a rich essence that has been further reduced and has sherry or Madeira wine added to it. Fumets and essences have the same uses.

Care after Preparation

Stocks must be handled with care because they are excellent media for bacterial growth. A stock should be cooled rapidly to below 45°F. Leaving it in the danger zone too long quickly produces a sour stock.

A stock is best cooled when transferred into small containers. Place the containers in an ice bath in the sink until the stock temperature is below 45°F. Then refrigerate or freeze it.

Soups

A good soup is made with quality ingredients and proper methods. One way to classify soups is according to consistency because this reflects their ingredients and dictates their use. Soups that cannot be classified this way are best classified according to their main ingredients.

A light soup should introduce a heavy meal. A heavier soup can precede a light meal or a sandwich or salad. Some heavy soups are meals in themselves. Many of these substantial soups are specialty or nationality soups.

Thin Soups

The thinnest soups are clear. Broths, bouillons, consommés, and other thin soups are made from clear stocks with only a few ingredients.

A **broth** is a rich, flavorful stock. A **bouillon** is made from stock, extra meat, and seasonings and is perhaps clarified. A bouillon has a fairly strong flavor of the main meat ingredient. A **consommé** is considered the perfect clear, thin soup. One makes it by clarifying a rich stock or broth, using added meat and flavoring ingredients. Other thin soups include light vegetable soup, milk or light cream soup, light bisque or puree soup, and some cold soups, such as vichyssoise.

Thick Soups

The difference between thin and thick soups is sometimes slight. A puree can be thin and light, or it can be quite heavy and thick. Some vegetable soups are very heavy because they contain many ingredients. Many heavy soups are thickened with rice, potatoes, macaroni, starch, or eggs. A chowder or gumbo also can be thickened by many ingredients.

Nationality and Specialty Soups

Nationality soups can be thick or thin. They form a separate category because of their specific ingredients, methods of preparation, or origins. French onion soup, the mulligatawny of India, Scotch broth with its typical barley, olla podrida of Spain, Russian borscht, and Italian minestrone fall into this category.

Many specialty soups are served cold—for example, delicate avocado soup seasoned with lemon and sherry, jellied madrilene, gazpacho, and chilled fruit soups.

Preparation of Soups

Quality ingredients and proper production techniques are very important in soup preparation. Attention must be given to the soup's consistency, seasoning, garnish, and special production needs.

Consistency

A thin soup may often be watery because the stock itself lacks enough body. Good body in stock results from an ample amount of the gelatin that comes from bones of young animals. Additional body can come from thickening agents, such as starches, rice, macaroni, potatoes, or pureed legumes. Meat, fish, poultry, and vegetables are also "body builders."

Seasoning

When soup is seasoned, the flavors should blend; as in a balanced musical ensemble, one element should not predominate. Adding spices and other seasonings toward the end of preparation ensures maximum flavor. Delicacy of seasoning is the key.

Garnish

A thin soup is often enriched by a garnish cut from the food item for which the soup is named. Creativity in soup garnishing, such as the use of sour cream, croutons, vegetable cuttings, and so on, is desired.

Special Procedures in Soup Production

The following are standard procedures for making a good soup.

1. Always skim the surface of the stock. Whenever you prepare a stock for soup production, skim off both fat and scum as they appear. This produces a clearer stock—and a better soup.
2. Strain your stocks and soups. You should strain all stocks after completion to remove impurities and obtain a clearer soup. Some soups—particularly thin ones—need to be strained through a china cap covered with cheesecloth. Bouillons, consommés, and other clear soups should be so clear that they sparkle.
3. Use spices with discretion. Subtle seasoning is the key. A stock or soup should be a blend of flavors. Some chefs remove the small round part of a clove because it can give a slight bitterness. Others crack whole peppercorns in order to extract more flavor. Spices should not be added unless in a sachet bag or bouquet garni. Spices should be in the stock or soup only long enough to contribute their flavor; then the sachet bag or bouquet garni should be removed.
4. Sauté vegetable garnishes for improved flavor. Some vegetables added to soups improve in flavor if sautéed first.

Care after Preparation

Most soups sour easily and must be handled just like stocks. Cool your soup quickly in a sink, and refrigerate it as soon as possible. A thick soup cools more quickly when stirred.

Carryover soups can have many uses. Many can be added to the stockpot—if they are the right kind. A soup can also be used as a base for other dishes. Often soups can be combined to make a new soup. For example, soup du jour can often be nothing more than "cream-of-yesterday's soup." A carryover cream of tomato soup blended with a carryover split pea soup makes a Mongole soup. A carryover cream of potato soup can readily be made into a potato soup à la Jackson.

You can plan a run-out time for soups to reduce carryovers. For backup you can always use one of the so-called "convenience soups." Many of these soups are of good quality and can be used in emergencies.

Basic White Stock

Yield: 1 gallon

INGREDIENTS NEEDED
2 lb chicken or knuckle of veal
1¼ qt cold water
2 peppercorns
1 clove
½ tsp sweet herbs
1 tbsp diced onion
1 tbsp diced celery
1 tsp salt

EQUIPMENT NEEDED
2-qt stockpot
Cutting board
French knife
China cap
Cheesecloth
Liquid and dry measures

PROCEDURE

1. Cut chicken into small pieces, add remaining ingredients, and simmer 2 to 3 hours.
2. Skim surface of stock during cooking process.
3. Strain through a china cap and cheesecloth.
4. Cool quickly, using an ice bath.
5. Remove fat from surface.
6. Reheat and serve hot.

Basic Brown Stock

Yield: 10 servings

INGREDIENTS NEEDED
5-lb beef soup bone
3 qt cold water
8 peppercorns
5 cloves
1 bay leaf
2 sprigs parsley
¼ tsp thyme
1 tbsp salt
1 stalk celery
½ c diced carrots
½ c diced turnips
2 large onions, sliced

EQUIPMENT NEEDED
2-gal stockpot
Liquid and dry measures
Cutting board
French knife
Cheesecloth
China cap

PROCEDURE

1. Cut lean meat from bones and brown one-third of it in marrow taken from bones.
2. Put remaining meat and bones in stockpot, cover with water, and let stand for 1 hour.
3. Add browned meat and seasonings, and bring to a boil. Reduce heat and let simmer for at least 1 hour.
4. Skim surface of soup during cooking process.
5. Add vegetables and cook 1 more hour.
6. Strain through china cap lined with cheesecloth and cool.
7. When cold, remove layer of fat that forms at top.

Savory Garden Soup

Yield: 4 servings

INGREDIENTS NEEDED
1 carrot, diced
½ small turnip, diced
⅓ c shredded white cabbage
1 tbsp butter
3 c soup stock
½ leek, sliced
½ c peas
1 tbsp salt
½ potato, diced
1 tsp minced parsley

EQUIPMENT NEEDED
Cutting board
Wet and dry measures
2-qt stockpot
French knife

PROCEDURE

1. Sauté carrot, turnip, and cabbage in butter in stockpot.
2. Add soup stock, leek, peas, salt, potato, and parsley.
3. Simmer for approximately 40 minutes.

Fresh Cabbage Soup

Yield: 6 to 8 servings

INGREDIENTS NEEDED
5 slices bacon, diced
1 lb white cabbage, chopped
2 carrots, sliced
2 potatoes, sliced
1 stalk celery, sliced
1½ qt water
2 tbsp flour
2 tbsp margarine (room temp.)
Salt and pepper

EQUIPMENT NEEDED
Cutting board
French knife
3-qt stockpot
Small sauté pan
Liquid and dry measures
Wire whip

PROCEDURE

1. Fry bacon until golden (but not crisp) in stockpot.
2. Add vegetables and water. Simmer for 30 minutes or until vegetables are tender.
3. Blend flour into margarine and stir into soup.
4. Bring soup to boiling point, stirring constantly.
5. Season to taste with salt and pepper.

Chilly Cucumber Soup

Yield: 4 servings

INGREDIENTS NEEDED

1 large cucumber, scored
¼ tsp salt
⅛ tsp pepper
1½ c plain yogurt
1¼ c water
½ c walnuts, ground
2 cloves garlic, minced
Green food coloring (optional)
4 large bowls of crushed ice

EQUIPMENT NEEDED

3-qt stockpot
Cutting board
French knife
6-oz ladle
Liquid and dry measures
Fork (for scoring cucumber)
Blender (for grinding walnuts)
Bowl with lid
4 soup bowls

PROCEDURE

1. Halve cucumber lengthwise, and cut crosswise into very thin slices.
2. Rub inside of bowl with cut surface of half a garlic clove.
3. Combine cucumber, salt, and pepper in bowl. Then cover and chill.
4. Combine yogurt and water. Pour over chilled cucumber and mix well. If desired, tint mixture with 1 or 2 drops of green food coloring.
5. Combine walnuts and garlic, and set aside for topping.
6. Ladle soup into bowls. Place soup bowls over larger bowls of crushed ice.
7. Serve with walnut topping.

Creamy Cheddar Cheese Soup

Yield: 2 quarts

INGREDIENTS NEEDED

2 tbsp butter or margarine
2 tbsp chopped onion
⅓ c all-purpose flour
1¼ tsp dry mustard
¼ tsp garlic powder
¼ tsp paprika
2 tsp Worcestershire sauce
1½ qt milk
3 tbsp chicken stock base
1½ c sliced celery
2½ c shredded cheddar cheese
Chopped green pepper
Cooked, crumbled bacon
Pimento strips
Toasted slivered almonds

EQUIPMENT NEEDED

3-qt stockpot
Cutting board
French knife
Liquid and dry measures
Hand grater
Wire whip

PROCEDURE

1. Melt butter or margarine in 3-quart stockpot. Add onion and sauté until tender. Stir in flour, mustard, garlic powder, paprika, and Worcestershire sauce.
2. Remove from heat; gradually add milk, stirring constantly.
3. Add chicken stock base and celery; mix well.
4. Cook over low heat, stirring occasionally, until thickened.
5. Add cheese, and stir until cheese is melted and soup reaches desired serving temperature. **Do not let soup boil at any time.**
6. Serve topped with your choice of green pepper, pimento, almonds, or bacon.

PRODUCT EVALUATION SHEET

Name _____   Lab date _____

Product prepared_____   Total prep time _____

Cooking method_____

Describe the following in one or two short sentences.

APPEARANCE (size, shape, consistency, etc.):

COLOR (golden brown, pasty white, bright, dull, etc.):

TEXTURE (smooth, lumpy, fine, coarse, sticky, gummy, etc.):

FLAVOR (sweet, sour, bitter, strong, spicy, bland, etc.):

TEMPERATURE (warm, hot, cold . . . Is it appropriate for the product?):

PROBLEMS ENCOUNTERED:

SOLUTION:
Suggestions to alter or improve the product:
1.

2.

Rating (10 being perfect):

0   1   2   3   4   5   6   7   8   9   10

10

Thickening Agents

To produce great sauces, you must first master preparation of thickening agents. A sauce must be thick enough to cling lightly to the food; otherwise it will just run off and lie in a puddle on the plate. But this doesn't mean that it should be heavy and pasty. Figure 10-1 shows how a thickening agent contributes to the structure of a finished sauce.

Starches as Thickeners

Starches are the most common thickening agents. Flour is the principal starch used in sauce making. Other thickening starches include cornstarch, arrowroot, bread crumbs, and other vegetable and grain products such as potato starch and rice flour.

Starches thicken by gelatinization, the process in which starch granules absorb water and swell to many times their original size. Because acids inhibit gelatinization, do not add acid ingredients to sauces until the starch has fully gelatinized.

Starch granules must be well separated before they are heated in liquid. If the granules are not separated, lumping occurs as the starch on the outside of the lump quickly gelatinizes into a coating and prevents the liquid from reaching the starch inside.

You can separate starch granules in two ways:

1. Mix the starch with fat. This is the principle of a roux.
2. Mix the starch with a cold liquid. This is the principle used with starches other than flour, such as cornstarch. A mixture of raw starch and cold liquid is called a **slurry**.

Another kind of starch can also be mixed with flour, but this makes an inferior sauce.

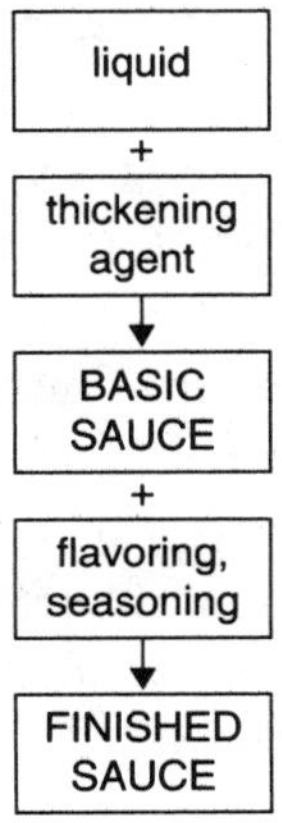

The Roux

Roux (pronounced "roo") is a cooked mixture of equal parts (by weight) of fat and flour.

liquid
+
thickening
agent
↓
BASIC
SAUCE
+
flavoring,
seasoning
↓
FINISHED
SAUCE

FIGURE 10-1   Structure of a Finished Sauce

Correct amounts of fat and flour are crucial to a good roux. There must be enough fat to coat all the starch granules, but not too much.

A good roux should be stiff, not runny or pourable. A roux with too much fat is called a slack roux. Using excess fat increases the cost of the roux unnecessarily; moreover, the excess fat rises to the top of the sauce, where it makes the sauce look greasy unless you skim it off.

Preparing a Roux

A roux must be cooked so that the finished sauce does not have the raw, starchy taste of the flour. There are three types of roux, each prepared in a different way.

1. **White roux** is cooked for just a few minutes—only until the raw taste is cooked out. Stop cooking as soon as the roux has a frothy, chalky, slightly gritty appearance, before it takes on color. White roux is used for béchamel and other white sauces based on milk.
2. **Blond roux** or **pale roux** is cooked a little longer, just until the roux begins to take on a slightly darker color. Blond roux is used for veloutés—sauces based on white stocks. These sauces have a pale ivory color.
3. **Brown roux** is cooked over low heat until it takes on a light brown color and a nutty aroma. Use low heat so that the roux browns easily without scorching. For a deeper brown roux, brown the flour in an oven before adding the fat. A heavily browned roux has only about a third of the thickening power of white roux, but it adds considerable flavor and color to brown sauces.

Incorporating the Roux

Combining roux with liquid to obtain a smooth, lump-free sauce is a skill that takes practice to master. The procedure is illustrated in Figure 10-2. Here are the general principles:

▼ Liquid may be added to roux, or roux may be added to liquid.

▼ The liquid may be hot or cold, but not ice cold. A very cold liquid will solidify the fat in the roux.

▼ The roux may be warm or cold, but not sizzling hot. Adding a hot liquid to a very hot roux causes splattering and, possibly, lumps.

▼ When preparing roux always use a stainless steel sauté pan rather than an aluminum pan because whipping in aluminum causes the roux to turn gray.

The method of **adding liquid to roux** is used when a roux is made up specifically for one sauce, gravy, or soup. Follow these procedures:

1. Use a heavy saucepan to avoid scorching either the roux or the sauce.
2. When the roux is made, remove the pan from the burner for a few minutes to cool slightly.
3. Slowly pour the liquid, continuously beating vigorously with a wire whip to prevent lumps from forming. If the liquid is hot, you will have to beat especially vigorously because the starch will gelatinize quickly. If the liquid is cool, you can add a portion of it, beat to dissolve the roux, then add the remainder of the liquid, hot or cold.
4. Bring the liquid to a boil, continuing to beat well. The roux does not reach its full thickening power until near the boiling point.
5. Simmer the sauce, stirring occasionally, until all the starch taste of the flour has been cooked out. This will take at least 10 minutes, but the flavor and consistency of the sauce will improve if it is cooked longer.
6. When the sauce is finished, it may be kept hot in a bain-marie or cooled for later use. Either way, you should cover the sauce or melt a thin film of butter onto the top to prevent a skin from forming.

Figure 10-3 shows the proportions of roux to liquid.

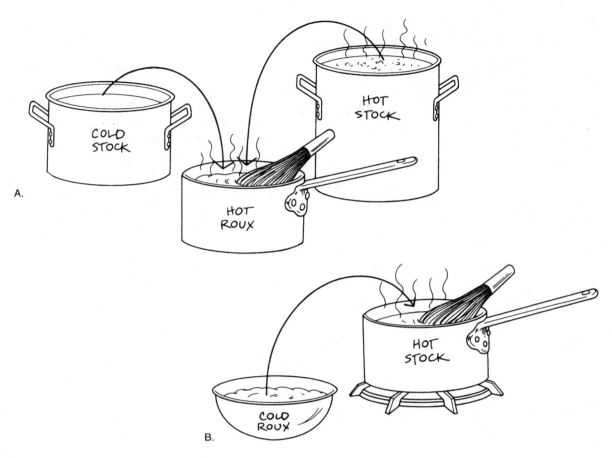

FIGURE 10-2   Roux Incorporation

Other Thickening Agents
Starch-Based Thickeners

Beurre manié (burr mahn-YAY) is a mixture of equal parts soft butter or margarine and flour worked together into a smooth paste. Use it for quick thickening at the end of cooking, to finish a sauce. The raw butter or margarine adds flavor and gives a sheen to the sauce when it melts. Drop very small pieces into a simmering sauce and stir with a whip until smooth. Repeat until the desired consistency is reached. Simmer just a few minutes more to cook the flour, and then remove the sauce from the heat.

Whitewash is a thin mixture of flour and cold water. Sauces made with whitewash have neither as good a flavor nor as fine a texture as those made with roux.

Cornstarch has roughly twice the thickening power of flour and produces a sauce that is almost clear, with a glossy texture. It is usually used in desserts. Mix cornstarch with cold water until smooth. Stir the mixture into the hot liquid. Bring to a boil and simmer until the liquid

SAUCE	BUTTER	FLOUR	ROUX	LIQUID
Thin or light	6 oz	6 oz	12 oz	1 gal
Medium	8 oz	8 oz	1 lb	1 gal
Thick or heavy	12 oz	12 oz	1½ lb	1 gal

FIGURE 10-3   Proportions of Roux to Liquid

turns clear and there is no starchy taste. **Do not boil for long, or the starch will break down and the liquid will thin out.** Sauces thickened with cornstarch may thin out if held on the steam table for long periods.

Arrowroot is used like cornstarch and yields an even clearer sauce. It is preferable, but its use is limited by its high cost—which elevates basic food cost.

Bread crumbs and other crumbs will thicken a liquid very quickly because they have already been cooked. Bread crumbs are useful when smoothness of texture is not desired.

The Liaison

The liaison, made of egg yolks and cream, is used primarily as a finishing touch to enhance flavor and smoothness of liquids. Egg yolks have the power to thicken a sauce slightly because egg proteins coagulate when heated. Pure egg yolks coagulate very fast; for this reason they are beaten with heavy cream before use. The heavy cream also adds thickness and flavor to the sauce. Use caution when thickening with egg yolks because of the danger of curdling, which occurs when the proteins coagulate too much and separate from the liquid.

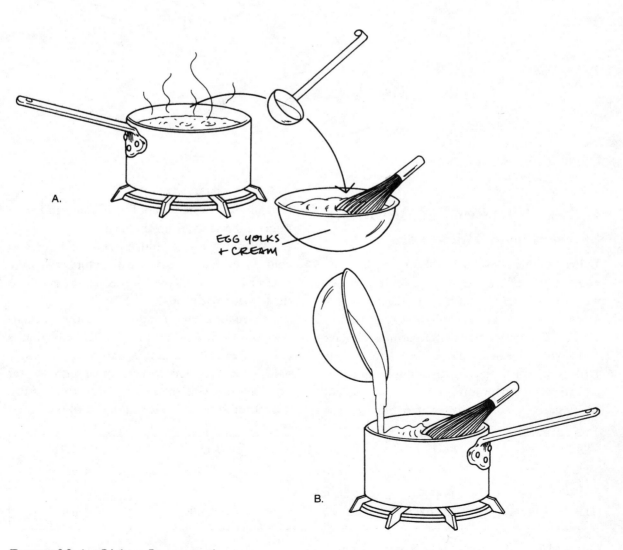

FIGURE 10-4   Liaison Incorporation

Egg yolks have only a slight thickening power. Liaisons produce only slight thickening. Remember: A liaison is used only as a finishing technique.

Following are the steps in preparing and incorporating a liaison:

1. Beat together egg yolks and cream in a stainless steel bowl. Normal proportions are 2 to 3 parts cream to 1 part egg yolks.
2. Very slowly add a little of the hot liquid to the liaison, beating constantly. This is known as tempering.
3. Off the heat, add the warmed, diluted liaison to the rest of the sauce, stirring well as you pour it in.
4. Return the sauce to low heat to warm it gently, but do not heat it higher than 180°F or it will curdle. **Never let it boil.**

Figure 10-4 shows how a liaison is incorporated into a liquid.

Basic Roux

INGREDIENTS NEEDED
8 oz flour
8 oz butter (or other animal fat) or margarine

EQUIPMENT NEEDED
Dry measures
Ounce scale
Stainless steel sauté pan
Wire whip

PROCEDURE

1. Premeasure ingredients, using an ounce scale.
2. Melt butter, margarine, or animal fat in the sauté pan at low temperature.
3. Beat the flour into melted fat until mixture is smooth and free from all lumps.
4. Remove from heat just as the roux is beginning to brown.

PRODUCT EVALUATION SHEET

Name _____   Lab date_____

Product prepared_____   Total prep time _____

Cooking method_____

Describe the following in one or two short sentences.

APPEARANCE (size, shape, consistency, etc.):

COLOR (golden brown, pasty white, bright, dull, etc.):

TEXTURE (smooth, lumpy, fine, coarse, sticky, gummy, etc.):

FLAVOR (sweet, sour, bitter, strong, spicy, bland, etc.):

TEMPERATURE (warm, hot, cold . . . Is it appropriate for the product?):

PROBLEMS ENCOUNTERED:

SOLUTION:
Suggestions to alter or improve the product:
1.

2.

Rating (10 being perfect):

0   1   2   3   4   5   6   7   8   9   10

11

Sauces

A sauce is a richly flavored, thickened liquid used to complement another dish. The sauce selected to accompany any dish should heighten its flavor, enhance its appearance, and make it more digestible. It should flow over the food and provide a thin coating, rather than disguise the dish itself. Preparing sauces gives you an opportunity to display your creative and imaginative skills. However, there are certain standards that must be met when you prepare a sauce.

The Functions of Sauces

Sauces add the following qualities to foods:
▼ Moistness
▼ Flavor
▼ Richness
▼ Appearance (color and shine)
▼ Interest and appetite appeal

The Structure of Sauces

Sauces are made of three kinds of ingredients:
▼ A liquid, the body of the sauce
▼ A thickening agent
▼ Additional seasoning and flavoring ingredients

A liquid ingredient provides the body or base of most sauces. There are five basic liquids on which most sauces are built. The five basic types of sauces are called the **leading sauces,** as shown in Figure 11-1.

The most frequently used sauces are based on stocks. The quality of these sauces is directly related to the preparation skills of the person making the stocks. Figure 11-2 details the composition of various types of sauces, and Figure 11-3 shows how basic sauces become finished sauces.

LIQUID	LEADING SAUCE
Milk	Béchamel sauce
White stock (veal, chicken, fish)	Velouté sauce
Brown stock	Brown sauce or Espagnole sauce
Tomato	Tomato sauce
Butter	Hollandaise sauce

FIGURE 11-1 The Leading Sauces

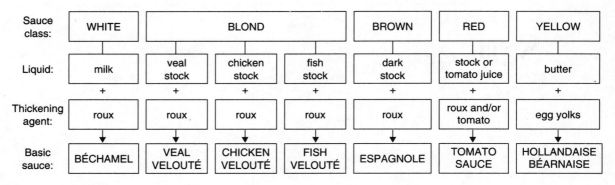

FIGURE 11-2   Ingredients of Sauces

Standards of Quality for Sauces

Good sauces meet the following standards of quality:

1. Consistency and body: Smooth with no lumps; not too thick or pasty, but thick enough to coat the food lightly.
2. Flavor: Distinctive but well balanced; proper degree of seasoning; no starch taste. The flavor should be selected to enhance or complement the food or to provide a pleasing contrast.
3. Appearance: Smooth, with a good shine; good color.

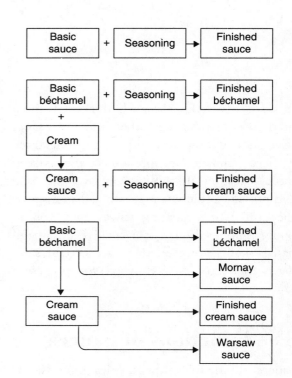

FIGURE 11-3   Finished Sauces

Béchamel Sauce

Yield: 1 gallon

INGREDIENTS NEEDED
8 oz butter or margarine
8 oz flour
1 gal milk
1 small whole onion, peeled
1 whole clove
1 bay leaf
½ tsp salt
⅛ tsp white pepper
Nutmeg to taste

EQUIPMENT NEEDED
2 heavy saucepans
Wire whip
Liquid and dry measures
Scale
China cap
Cheesecloth

PROCEDURE

1. Heat butter in heavy pot over low heat. Add flour and make a white roux. Cool roux slightly.
2. In another saucepan, scald the milk. Gradually add it to roux, beating constantly.
3. Bring sauce to a boil, stirring constantly. Reduce heat to a simmer.
4. Attach bay leaf to onion with clove and add to sauce. Simmer at least 15 minutes. Stir.
5. Adjust consistency with more hot milk if necessary.
6. Season very lightly with salt, nutmeg, and white pepper. Spice flavors should not dominate.
7. Strain sauce through china cap lined with cheesecloth. Cover, or spread melted butter on surface to prevent skin formation. Keep hot in bain-marie, or cool in cold water bath.

Velouté Sauce (Veal, Chicken, or Fish)

Yield: 1 gallon

INGREDIENTS NEEDED
8 oz clarified butter
8 oz bread flour
5 qt veal, chicken, or fish stock, heated

EQUIPMENT NEEDED
2-gal stockpot
Wire whip
China cap
Cheesecloth
Liquid and dry measures
Scale

PROCEDURE

1. Heat butter in stockpot over low heat. Add flour and make a blond roux. Cool roux slightly.
2. Gradually add hot stock to roux, beating constantly. Bring to a boil, stirring constantly. Reduce heat to a simmer.
3. Simmer sauce very slowly for an hour. Stir occasionally, and skim surface when necessary. Add more stock if needed to adjust consistency.
4. Do not season velouté. It is not used as is but as an ingredient in other preparations.
5. Strain through china cap lined with cheesecloth. Cover or spread melted butter on surface to prevent skin formation. Keep hot in a bain-marie, or cool in a cold water bath for later use.

Espagnole Sauce (Brown Sauce)

Yield: 5 quarts

INGREDIENTS NEEDED

1 lb medium onions, diced medium
½ lb celery, diced medium
½ lb carrots, diced medium
10 oz butter or margarine
10 oz bread flour
5 qt brown stock, hot
8 oz tomato puree
1 bay leaf
Salt to taste
Pepper to taste

EQUIPMENT NEEDED

Cutting board
French knife
Liquid and dry measures
Scale
Wire whip
2-gal stockpot
China cap
Cheesecloth

PROCEDURE

1. Sauté all vegetables in butter or margarine in stockpot until onions are transparent.
2. Add flour and cook 10 minutes.
3. Add **hot** brown stock and tomato puree, stirring until slightly thickened and smooth.
4. Add bay leaf, salt, and pepper and cool 1½ hours.
5. Adjust for flavor and consistency.
6. Strain through china cap lined with cheesecloth.

Tomato Sauce

Yield: 2 gallons

INGREDIENTS NEEDED

1 pt salad oil
2 lb onions, chopped fine
½ lb celery, chopped fine
2 oz green pepper, chopped fine
1 lb pork bones
5 tbsp garlic, minced
2 #10 cans Italian tomatoes, crushed
1 #10 can tomato puree
2 tsp basil leaves, crushed
3 tbsp oregano leaves
2 tbsp salt
2 tsp pepper
1 qt water

EQUIPMENT NEEDED

Cutting board
French knife
Liquid and dry measures
Can opener
3-gal stockpot
Rubber spatula
Large spoon for stirring

PROCEDURE

1. Sauté onions, celery, green peppers, and pork bones in salad oil for about 15 minutes, stirring frequently. Make sure onions are transparent and pork bones are browned.
2. Add garlic and cook for approximately 3 more minutes.
3. Add tomatoes, tomato puree, and water. Use rubber spatula to clean out cans thoroughly. Add remaining ingredients.
4. Simmer uncovered for at least 2 hours, stirring frequently.
5. Remove pork bones before serving.

Hollandaise Sauce

Yield: 1 quart

INGREDIENTS NEEDED
1 lb butter
8 egg yolks
½ lemon
Salt to taste
Tabasco sauce to taste

EQUIPMENT NEEDED
1-qt stainless steel bowl
French whip
Liquid measures
Double boiler

PROCEDURE

1. Melt butter.
2. Break eggs and separate whites from yolks. Reserve whites for other preparations.
3. Squeeze juice from ½ lemon.
4. Place water in double boiler and bring to a boil.
5. Put egg yolks in bowl, add a few drops of water (approximately ½ teaspoon), and mix well.
6. Put bowl in hot water when temperature of double boiler cools to approximately 160°F.
7. Beat yolks slowly with French whip until they foam and tighten.
8. Remove from water and add melted butter very slowly, whipping continuously with French whip.
9. When all butter is added, forming an emulsion, season with salt, Tabasco sauce, and lemon juice.

Be very careful that the water is not too hot, or the eggs will coagulate.
Whip continuously throughout the entire preparation process.

Mock Hollandaise Sauce

Compare the taste and consistency of this mock hollandaise sauce with the true hollandaise sauce on the previous page.

Yield: 1 quart

INGREDIENTS NEEDED
1 large lemon
2 qt milk
10 egg yolks
8 oz butter
6 oz all-purpose flour
Salt and pepper to taste
Yellow food coloring, if desired
Tabasco sauce to taste

EQUIPMENT NEEDED
Quart liquid measure
Ounce scale
2 4-qt saucepans
Wire whip
Stainless steel bowl
Cup liquid measures

PROCEDURE

Have all your ingredients and equipment within reach during this preparation process.

1. Squeeze juice from lemon.
2. Heat milk in one saucepan. Use low heat so scorching will not occur.
3. Separate eggs. Reserve whites for other preparations.
4. Place butter in other saucepan, and melt.
5. Add flour, making a roux, and cook for 3 minutes.
6. Add hot milk, whipping vigorously with wire whip. Allow mixture to simmer for 5 minutes.
7. Place egg yolks in stainless steel bowl, and beat with wire whip. Drip in a small amount of hot cream sauce and blend with egg yolks. Slowly pour this mixture into simmering cream sauce, mixing continuously.
8. Add lemon juice and season with salt, pepper, and tabasco to taste.
9. Tint with yellow food color if desired.

When adding egg yolks to the cream sauce, pour very slowly and whip briskly.
Be careful not to scorch the sauce.

PRODUCT EVALUATION SHEET

Name _____ Lab date _____

Product prepared_____ Total prep time _____

Cooking method_____

Describe the following in one or two short sentences.

APPEARANCE (size, shape, consistency, etc.):

COLOR (golden brown, pasty white, bright, dull, etc.):

TEXTURE (smooth, lumpy, fine, coarse, sticky, gummy, etc.):

FLAVOR (sweet, sour, bitter, strong, spicy, bland, etc.):

TEMPERATURE (warm, hot, cold . . . Is it appropriate for the product?):

PROBLEMS ENCOUNTERED:

SOLUTION:
Suggestions to alter or improve the product:
1.

2.

Rating (10 being perfect):

0   1   2   3   4   5   6   7   8   9   10

Vegetables

Vegetable Classifications

Vegetables are usually classified according to the parts of the plant from which they are taken, such as roots, stalks, leaves, and so on (see Fig. 12-1).

Root vegetables. Potatoes, carrots, and turnips. They are usually starchy because the root is the storehouse of energy to grow the new plant.

Bulb vegetables. Onions, garlic, and shallots. They are related to the lily family and often are

BULBS	FRUITS	FLOWERS	ROOTS
Chives	Cucumbers	Artichokes	Beets
Onions	Eggplant	Broccoli	Parsnips
Garlic	Tomatoes	Brussels sprouts	Potatoes
Leeks	Okra	Cauliflower	Rutabagas
Shallots	Peppers		Radishes
	Squash		Turnips
			Sweet potatoes
			Carrots

LEAVES	STALKS	SEEDS AND PODS
Brussels sprouts	Asparagus	Beans
Cabbage	Celery	Green beans
Chinese cabbage	Peas	Peas
Chard	Corn	
Endive	Rhubarb	
Kale		
Lettuce		
Mustard greens		
Romaine		
Spinach		
Watercress		

FIGURE 12-1 Common Vegetables Classified as Parts of the Plant

considered herbs. They generally have a strong taste and odor and are used to add flavor to many dishes.

Stalk vegetables. Asparagus, rhubarb, and celery. They must be young and succulent.

Leaf vegetables. Spinach, lettuce, chard, and romaine. Usually used as the base for salads, they must be young. Old plants are very tough.

Flower vegetables. Cauliflower, brussels sprouts, and broccoli. They are picked before full flowering.

Seed and pod vegetables. Peas, beans, and corn. Green peas and beans are picked before they are fully ripe. Corn also is more flavorful and tender if not fully ripe. Corn may be cooked and served on the cob or stripped from the cob.

Fruit vegetables. Squash, tomatoes, and eggplant.

In terms of flavor, vegetables are grouped as either mild or strong. The strong-flavored vegetables include those with a cabbagelike flavor, such as brussels sprouts, turnips, and cauliflower, and those with an onionlike flavor, such as leeks and garlic. Most other vegetables are considered mild in flavor.

Controlling Quality Changes during Cooking

Many guides to vegetable cookery simply present you with long, boring lists of rules. Instead of memorizing rules, you can understand principles if you first learn

▼ What happens—how vegetables change as they are cooked and
▼ How to affect what happens—how to control those changes.

Cooking affects vegetables in four ways. It changes the texture, flavor, color, and nutrient content. How much these four characteristics change determines whether your final product will be attractive and delicious or end up in your garbage can. You can control these changes if you understand how they happen.

Controlling Texture Changes

Changing the texture is one of the main purposes of cooking vegetables. Cooking affects fiber and starch, two components that determine the texture of vegetables.

Fiber

Vegetable fiber is mostly cellulose and pectin. The fiber structure gives vegetables shape and firmness; cooking softens the fibers.

The amount of fiber in vegetables varies a great deal . . .
▼ In different vegetables. Spinach and tomatoes have less fiber than carrots and turnips.
▼ In different examples of the same vegetable. Old, tough carrots have more fiber than young, fresh carrots.
▼ In different parts of the same vegetable. The tender tips of asparagus and broccoli have less fiber than their tougher stalks.

Fiber is made firmer by . . .
▼ Acids. Lemon juice, vinegar, and tomato products, when added to cooking vegetables, extend the cooking time.
▼ Sugars. Sugar strengthens cellulose. You will use this principle primarily in fruit cookery. For firm poached apples or pears, for example, cook in a heavy syrup. For applesauce, cook apples until soft before sweetening.

Fiber is softened by . . .
▼ Heat. In general, longer cooking means softer vegetables.
▼ Alkalis. Do not add baking soda to green vegetables. Not only does it destroy vitamins, but it makes the vegetables unpleasantly mushy.

Starch

Starch granules give vegetables texture and flavor.
▼ Dry starch foods like dried legumes (beans, peas, lentils), rice, and pasta must be cooked in enough water that the starch granules can absorb moisture and soften.

Dried beans are usually soaked before cooking to replace lost moisture.

▼ Most starchy vegetables like potatoes and yams have enough moisture of their own, but they still must be cooked until the starch granules soften.

Achieving Proper Doneness

A vegetable is done when it has reached the desired degree of tenderness. This stage varies from vegetable to vegetable. Most, however, are best when cooked very briefly, only until they are crisp-tender. At this stage of tenderness they have not only a most pleasing texture but also maximum flavor, color, and nutrients.

Follow these guidelines to achieve proper doneness in vegetables.

▼ Don't overcook vegetables.

▼ Cook as close to serving time as possible. If vegetables must be cooked in advance, slightly undercook them, cool them rapidly in cold water, drain and refrigerate, then reheat to order. Holding vegetables in a steam table continues to cook them.

▼ For uniform doneness, cut into uniform pieces before cooking.

▼ Vegetables with both tough and tender parts need special treatment, so that the tender parts are not overcooked by the time the tougher parts are done. For example, peel the woody stalks of asparagus, peel or split broccoli stalks, and pierce the base of brussels sprouts with a sharp knife.

▼ Don't cook different kinds of vegetables together. They probably need to be cooked to slightly different doneness.

You will want your cooked vegetables to meet the following standards of quality:

▼ Color. Colors should be bright and natural. Green vegetables, in particular, should be a fresh, bright green, not olive green or yellowish.

▼ Appearance on plate. Vegetables should be arranged attractively for presentation. Vegetables should be cut neatly and uniformly, not broken up. Excess cooking liquid should be reserved in the kitchen. Imaginative and appropriate combinations and garnishes should be used for eye appeal.

▼ Texture. Vegetables must be cooked to the right degree of doneness. Most vegetables should be crisp-tender; not overcooked and mushy but not tough or woody either. Vegetables that are intended to be soft (for instance, squash, yams, tomatoes, vegetable purees) should be cooked through, with a pleasant, smooth texture.

▼ Flavor. Vegetables should have full, natural flavor and sweetness, sometimes called "garden fresh" flavor. Strong-flavored vegetables should be pleasantly mild, with no off taste or bitterness.

▼ Seasonings. Vegetables should be lightly and appropriately seasoned. Seasonings should not be so strong that they mask the natural "garden" flavors.

▼ Sauces. Butter, whether ordinary or seasoned, should be fresh and used lightly; vegetables should not be greasy. Cream sauces and other sauces should not be too thick or too heavily seasoned. Like seasonings, sauces should enhance, not cover up.

▼ Combinations. Interesting vegetable combinations should be used to attract customers. Flavors, colors, and shapes should be pleasing in combination. Vegetables should be cooked separately and then combined, to allow for different cooking times. Acid vegetables (like tomatoes) added to green vegetables will discolor them; combine just before serving.

Handling Frozen Vegetables
Checking Quality

Examine all frozen products when they are received to make sure there has been no loss of quality. Check the following in particular:

▼ Temperature. Check the temperature inside the case with a thermometer. Has the product begun to thaw during shipment? It should be 0°F internally.

▼ Presence of large ice crystals. A little frost is normal, but lots of ice means poor handling.

▼ Signs of leaking on the carton. This is another obvious sign of thawing.

▼ Freezer burn. Open a package and check the vegetables themselves. Is the color bright and natural, or is there any yellowing or drying on the surface?

Cooking

Cook from the frozen state. Most vegetables need no thawing but can go directly into steamer pans or boiling salted water. Remember that frozen vegetables have been partially cooked, and final cooking time is usually cut in half. Salt is usually added during par-cooking, so cut salt in half during the preparation process.

Handling Canned Vegetables

Checking Quality

Like frozen vegetables, canned products should be inspected when you receive them.

▼ Reject damaged cans immediately. Puffed or swollen cans indicate spoilage. Small dents may be harmless, but large dents may damage the can's protective lining (K-Enamel). Do not accept rusted or leaking cans.

▼ Know the drained weight. This varies with different grades of different vegetables and should be specified when you order. Typical drained weights are 60 to 65 percent of total contents. You must know the drained weight to calculate the number of servings in the can. (Some canned products, such as tomato sauce or cream-style corn, have no drained weight because the entire contents are served.)

▼ Check the grade. Grades, which are determined by packers or federal inspectors, are based on factors like color, absence of defects, and sieve size. Check to make sure you receive the grade that you ordered. (See *Wenzel's Menu Maker* by George L. Wenzel, Boston, CBI Publishing Co., © 1979, for grades and selection.)

Cooking

▼ Wipe the top of the can clean before opening. Use a clean can opener.

▼ Drain the vegetables, and place half the liquid in the pot. Bring to a boil. This shortens the heating time for canned vegetables.

▼ Add the vegetables and heat only to serving temperature. Do not boil!

▼ Heat as close to serving time as possible. Do not hold vegetables in steam table pans for long periods—never longer than an hour.

▼ Season and flavor.

Methods of Vegetable Cookery

Boiling

Boiling is suitable for all vegetables and is the preferred method of cooking. The vegetable is added to a small amount of boiling water, covered, and quickly returned to a boil. Then the heat is reduced so that the water simmers gently.

To further preserve the color of bright green vegetables, cook them without a cover for the first few minutes. Baking soda should not be used to preserve color because it will destroy vitamins and cause excess fiber breakdown. Vegetables should be cooked only until they are fork-tender, or al dente.

Steaming

Steaming vegetables in a conventional steamer is much faster than boiling because the cooking temperature is higher. But it shouldn't be so high that the outside of the vegetable is overcooked before the inside is done.

▼ Use a perforated hotel pan for a more even distribution of steam during the cooking process, along with less breakage during the transfer to steam table for holding.

▼ To allow steam to circulate properly, do not overload the pan during the cooking process.

▼ When using the steamer, watch the time carefully to avoid overcooking. The temperature at 5 pounds of pressure should be 228°F.

▼ See the steamer equipment manual for proper vegetable cooking times and settings.

▼ Season creatively before serving.

Deep-Frying

Deep-fried vegetables may be divided into four categories:

▼ Vegetables dipped in batter and fried

▼ Vegetables breaded and fried

▼ Vegetables fried without a coating (for example, french fried potatoes; see Figure 12-2)

▼ Small vegetables or cut vegetables mixed with a batter and dropped into hot fat

Follow these procedures for deep-frying vegetables:

1. Assemble all equipment and food products.

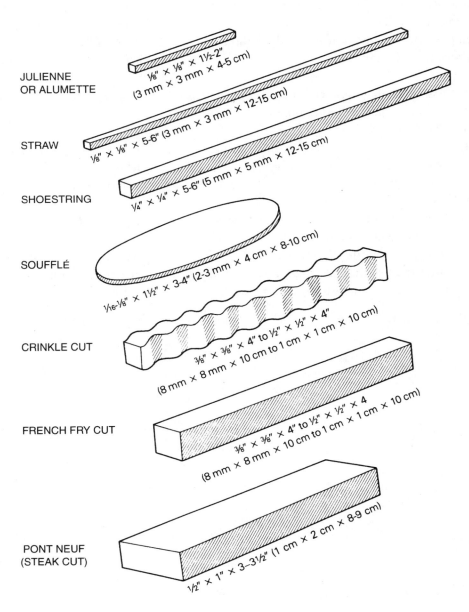

JULIENNE OR ALUMETTE ⅛" × ⅛" × 1½-2" (3 mm × 3 mm × 4-5 cm)

STRAW ⅛" × ⅛" × 5-6" (3 mm × 3 mm × 12-15 cm)

SHOESTRING ¼" × ¼" × 5-6" (5 mm × 5 mm × 12-15 cm)

SOUFFLÉ ¹⁄₁₆-⅛" × 1½" × 3-4" (2-3 mm × 4 cm × 8-10 cm)

CRINKLE CUT ⅜" × ⅜" × 4" to ½" × ½" × 4" (8 mm × 8 mm × 10 cm to 1 cm × 1 cm × 10 cm)

FRENCH FRY CUT ⅜" × ⅜" × 4" to ½" × ½" × 4 (8 mm × 8 mm × 10 cm to 1 cm × 1 cm × 10 cm)

PONT NEUF (STEAK CUT) ½" × 1" × 3-3½" (1 cm × 2 cm × 8-9 cm)

FIGURE 12-2   Potato Cuts

2. Preheat the fryer to the proper temperature, 325°F

3. Prepare food items as required.

4. Place the proper amount of food in the fryer—do not overload the basket.

5. Fry only until the desired doneness is achieved.

6. Remove the food from the fryer and let it drain.

7. Serve immediately.

Sautéing

Sautéing is a method for precooking or blanching vegetables. It is also a preferred method for cooking tender, small cuts of vegetables that might otherwise cook too quickly. Follow these procedures for sautéing:

1. Assemble all equipment and food products.

2. Prepare vegetables as required.

3. Place sauté pan on high heat.

4. When the pan is hot, add a small amount of clarified butter, oil, or other fat—enough to coat the bottom of the pan.

5. As soon as the fat is hot, add the vegetables. Do not overload the pan, or the temperature will be lowered and the vegetables will simmer rather than sauté.

6. After the heat has had time to recover, flip the pan a few times to turn and toss the vegetables. Let the pan sit again over the heat.

7. Continue to flip the vegetables as often as necessary for them to cook or heat evenly and become coated with the cooking fat.

8. As soon as the vegetables are cooked or heated through, remove from the pan and serve.

VEGETABLE PREPARATION TERMS

Blanch: To cook partially by scalding

Chop: To cut food into small, uneven pieces

Corrugated: Knife blade with curved ridges and hollows on its cutting edge

Dice: To cut food into cube-shaped pieces

Julienne: To cut food into long, thin strips

Legumes: Dried vegetables, such as beans, peas, or lentils

Mince: To cut food into very fine, unevenly shaped pieces

Pallet: Portable platform used for storage of cartons in a storeroom

Score: To make shallow slits in the surface of a food item

Slice: To cut food into relatively thin, broad pieces

Deep-Fried Zucchini

Yield: 6 servings

INGREDIENTS NEEDED
1¼ c all-purpose flour
1 tsp salt
¼ tsp pepper
2 eggs, well beaten
¾ c milk
1 tsp Worcestershire sauce
1 tbsp butter or margarine
2 lb zucchini, cut in ½-in. sticks
Grated Parmesan cheese

EQUIPMENT NEEDED
Cutting board
French knife
Liquid and dry measures
French fryer set at 325°F
Wire whip
Drain board
Cooking fork
Absorbent paper (paper towels)
Stainless steel bowl

PROCEDURE

1. Blend flour, salt, and pepper in bowl. Add a mixture of eggs, milk, Worcestershire sauce, and melted butter; beat with wire whip until smooth.
2. Preheat oil in fryer to 325°F.
3. Dip zucchini sticks in batter, using fork to coat evenly. Allow any excess coating to drip off.
4. Fry 2 to 3 minutes or until golden brown. Lift from oil and drain a few seconds before removing to absorbent paper.
5. Sprinkle with salt and grated Parmesan cheese.

Stir-Fry Vegetables and Rice

Yield: 6 to 8 servings

INGREDIENTS NEEDED
1 c brown rice
⅓ c vegetable oil
1 medium onion, thinly sliced
1 c thinly sliced carrots
1 clove garlic, crushed
1 green pepper, coarsely chopped
1 c thinly sliced zucchini
1 c thinly sliced mushrooms
2 cans (16 oz) bean sprouts, drained
¼ c soy sauce

EQUIPMENT NEEDED
Cutting board
French knife
Liquid and dry measures
Sauté pan
Small stockpot with lid

PROCEDURE

1. Cook rice according to the package directions; set aside to cool.
2. Heat oil in large sauté pan. Add onion, carrots, and crushed garlic; cook and stir over medium-high heat about 2 minutes.
3. Add green pepper, zucchini, and mushrooms; cook and stir 2 to 3 minutes.
4. Stir in cooked rice, bean sprouts, and soy sauce. Cook and stir 1 to 2 minutes or until thoroughly heated.

Stuffed Green Peppers

Yield: 4 servings

INGREDIENTS NEEDED

4 medium green peppers
¼ c vegetable oil
1 onion, finely chopped
2 cloves garlic, minced
½ lb ground beef
½ tsp salt
½ tsp pepper
½ tsp thyme
½ c drained stewed tomatoes
1 c cooked rice
1 tbsp parsley

EQUIPMENT NEEDED

Cutting board
French knife
Paring knife
Wet and dry measures
Small stockpot with lid
Small sauté pan
Large stainless steel bowl
Baking pan
Oven, preheated to 325°F

PROCEDURE

1. Cut top from each pepper, and remove seeds and veins. Blanch peppers and tops in boiling water for 3 to 4 minutes. Remove and let cool thoroughly.
2. In sauté pan, heat oil, add onion and garlic, and sauté for 4 to 5 minutes.
3. Add meat, salt, pepper, and thyme; cook until meat is browned.
4. In large bowl, combine meat mixture, tomatoes, rice, and parsley.
5. Stuff each pepper with meat mixture, place top back on each, and bake at 325°F for 20 to 25 minutes.

Scalloped Potatoes and Ham

Yield: 6 servings

INGREDIENTS NEEDED

¾ lb ham, cut in small cubes
1 tbsp vegetable oil
2 tbsp flour
2 c milk
8 medium potatoes, sliced thin
1 tsp salt
⅛ tsp pepper

EQUIPMENT NEEDED

Cutting board
French knife
Liquid and dry measures
Potato peeler
Small sauté pan
Small stockpot
2-qt hotel pan
Oven, preheated to 325°F

PROCEDURE

1. Lightly brown ham in sauté pan with vegetable oil. Blend in flour.
2. Heat milk in stockpot until boiling; add ham and potatoes, and reheat to boiling point.
3. Add salt and pepper.
4. Place in greased hotel pan. Bake at 325°F for 30 to 45 minutes, until potatoes are tender.

Mushrooms Parmesan

Yield: 6 to 8 servings

INGREDIENTS NEEDED

1 lb mushrooms (2-in. caps)
4 tbsp vegetable oil
¼ c chopped onion
½ clove garlic, finely chopped
⅓ c fine bread crumbs
3 tbsp Parmesan cheese
1 tbsp chopped parsley
½ tsp salt
⅛ tsp oregano

EQUIPMENT NEEDED

Cutting board
Paring knife
French knife
Shallow hotel pan
Sauté pan
Liquid and dry measures
Colander
Tablespoon
Oven, preheated to 400°F

PROCEDURE

1. Clean mushrooms and remove stems. Place caps, open end up, in greased hotel pan; set aside.
2. Finely chop mushroom stems.
3. Heat 2 tablespoons of vegetable oil in sauté pan. Add mushroom stems, onion, and garlic. Cook slowly until onion and garlic are slightly brown.
4. Combine bread crumbs, cheese, parsley, salt, and oregano. Mix in onion, garlic, and mushroom stems.
5. Lightly fill mushroom caps with mixture, using tablespoon.
6. Pour 2 tablespoons of vegetable oil into hotel pan.
7. Bake at 400°F 15 to 20 minutes, or until mushrooms are tender and tops are browned.

Cabbage Rolls Paprikash

Yield: 4 servings

INGREDIENTS NEEDED

8 large cabbage leaves
1½ c diced cooked chicken
2 tbsp chopped onion
½ c celery, chopped fine
¼ lb fresh mushrooms, chopped
1 small clove garlic, minced
½ tsp salt
1½ tsp thyme
1 egg, beaten
2 tbsp margarine
6 tbsp flour
2 c chicken stock, rich
2 c sour cream
3 tbsp paprika

EQUIPMENT NEEDED

Cutting board
French knife
Small stockpot
Wire whip
Liquid and dry measures
Rubber spatula
Shallow hotel pan
Sauté pan
Aluminum foil
Wooden toothpicks
Oven, preheated to 350°F

PROCEDURE

1. Cook cabbage leaves 4 minutes in boiling salted water to cover. Drain and pat dry.
2. Mix chicken, onion, celery, mushrooms, garlic, salt, and thyme; stir in egg.
3. Place ½ cup of chicken mixture in center of each cabbage leaf. Fold sides of cabbage leaf toward center, over filling, and then fold and overlap ends to make a small bundle.
4. Fasten with toothpicks. Place in hotel pan.
5. Heat margarine in sauté pan. Blend in flour, and heat until bubbly. Add chicken stock gradually, stirring until smooth. Blend in sour cream and paprika.
6. Cook over low heat, stirring constantly, until thickened. Pour sauce over cabbage rolls.
7. Cover hotel pan with aluminum foil and bake at 350°F for 35 to 40 minutes.

PRODUCT EVALUATION SHEET

Name _____   Lab date _____

Product prepared_____   Total prep time _____

Cooking method_____

Describe the following in one or two short sentences.

APPEARANCE (size, shape, consistency, etc.):

COLOR (golden brown, pasty white, bright, dull, etc.):

TEXTURE (smooth, lumpy, fine, coarse, sticky, gummy, etc.):

FLAVOR (sweet, sour, bitter, strong, spicy, bland, etc.):

TEMPERATURE (warm, hot, cold . . . Is it appropriate for the product?):

PROBLEMS ENCOUNTERED:

SOLUTION:
Suggestions to alter or improve the product:
1.

2.

Rating (10 being perfect):

0   1   2   3   4   5   6   7   8   9   10

13

Rice

Market Forms

In nature there are basically two varieties of rice; each one cooks up differently. **Long-grain rice** (probably discovered along a river in what is now Pakistan) becomes light and fluffy, with separate distinct grains. **Pearl** or **round rice** (probably discovered in China) cooks into a moist, sticky product. This variety is also called short- or medium-grain rice. Other popular terms relate to differences in processing.

Regular white rice or **polished rice** is rice that has been milled to remove the hull, the germ, and practically all of the bran. Unfortunately, milling also removes some of the vitamins and minerals. Then it is often polished with glucose and talc to improve its luster; hence the name polished rice. It has a bland flavor and tender texture.

Enriched rice is white rice that contains added vitamins and iron. Many processes have been tried in efforts to enrich rice, but most have proven unsuccessful because of nutrient loss during washing, cooking, and storage.

Parboiled rice is treated in a special steam-pressure process before milling. This process forces the vitamins and minerals from the hull, bran, and germ into the starchy part of the grain (called the *endosperm*). Much of the natural vitamin and mineral content is retained after milling. Parboiled rice takes longer to cook than regular white rice. The cooked grains are fluffy,

separate, and plump. **Converted rice** is parboiled rice made by a patented process. It has a creamy color but is not as fluffy as regular white rice.

Packaged precooked rice is long-grain white rice that has been cooked and dried. It takes less preparation time than regular white rice, but it costs more. It has a porous structure that permits rapid rehydration.

Brown rice is whole-grain rice from which the hull and a small amount of the bran have been removed. More nutritious than other forms of rice, it has a nutlike flavor and a slightly chewy texture. Brown rice needs to cook a little longer than regular white rice.

Wild rice isn't rice at all but the seed of a grass that grows wild in shallow lakes and marshes. It is dark brown, has a distinctive flavor, and costs considerably more than other types of rice. Like other whole grains, it has a relatively poor keeping quality, especially in warm weather.

Figure 13-1 gives approximate cooking times and yields for various kinds of rice.

Handling and Storage

Regular milled rice should be rinsed in cold water before boiling or steaming. This removes excess starch, which makes rice sticky. The rice industry recommends not washing rice because

TYPE	DRY AMOUNT	WATER AMOUNT	BOIL TIME	BAKE TIME	YIELD
Polished white rice	1 c	2 c	15 to 20 min	25 min	3 c
Enriched white rice	1 c	2 c	15 to 20 min	25 min	3 c
Parboiled/converted rice	1 c	2 c	20 to 25 min	30 to 40 min	3 to 4 c
Precooked rice	1 c	2 c	20 to 25 min	30 to 40 min	2 to 3 c
Brown rice	1 c	3 c	40 to 45 min	60 min	4 c
Long-grain wild rice	1 c	3 c	30 to 45 min	45 to 60 min	4 c

FIGURE 13-1   Rice Yields and Cooking Times

washing removes some of the vitamin coating of enriched rice. Do not buy low-grade rice, which tends to be dirty, or rice that has been coated with talc.

Store raw rice at room temperature in a dry place and in a tightly sealed container to keep out moisture and insects. White rice will keep for many months; brown rice is somewhat more perishable.

Cooking Procedures

Following are basic procedures for preparing plain boiled or steamed rice on top of the range, in the oven, or in the steamer.

Range-Top Method

1. Combine all ingredients in a heavy pot. Bring to a boil. Stir. Cover and cook over very low heat, observing these cooking times:
   — Long- and medium-grain rice—15 to 20 minutes
   — Parboiled rice—20 to 25 minutes
   — Brown rice— 40 to 45 minutes

2. Test the rice for doneness. Cook 2 to 4 minutes more if necessary.

3. Turn the rice out into a hotel pan. Fluff it with a fork or slotted spoon to let the steam escape.

Oven Method

1. Bring salted water to a boil. Combine all ingredients in a shallow steamer pan. Cover with foil or a tight lid. Place in 375°F oven. Use these cooking times:
   — Long- and medium-grain rice—25 minutes
   — Parboiled rice—30–40 minutes
   — Brown rice—1 hour

2. Test the rice for doneness. Bake 2 to 4 minutes more if necessary.

3. Fluff the rice with a fork or slotted spoon to let the steam escape.

Steamer Method

1. Bring salted water to a boil. Combine all ingredients in a shallow pan. Place uncovered pan in steamer for cooking time recommended by equipment manufacturer. Cooking times depend on type of steamer.

2. Test the rice for doneness. Steam 2 to 4 minutes more if necessary.

3. Fluff the rice with a fork or slotted spoon to let the steam escape.

Spanish Rice

Yield: 6 servings

INGREDIENTS NEEDED
6 slices bacon, chopped
1 onion, finely chopped
1½ lb ground beef
1 tsp salt
1 c uncooked rice
4 c tomato juice, heated
1 tsp paprika

EQUIPMENT NEEDED
Cutting board
French knife
Sauté pan
Liquid and dry measures
Shallow hotel pan
Colander
Oven, preheated to 350°F

PROCEDURE

1. Sauté bacon slowly and pour off part of fat.
2. Brown chopped onion and beef in hot fat. Add salt.
3. Wash rice, drain, and add with 1½ cups tomato juice and paprika to meat.
4. Pour into greased hotel pan and bake at 350°F until rice is tender, approximately 30 minutes.
5. Add more tomato juice if needed during baking process.
6. **Do not let rice dry out.**

Chicken and Brown Rice

Yield: 6 servings

INGREDIENTS NEEDED
3½ lb chicken, 8 cut
2 tbsp salt
1 c diced celery
3 qt boiling water
1 c uncooked brown rice

EQUIPMENT NEEDED
Cutting board
French knife
Liquid and dry measures
Heavy pot

PROCEDURE

1. Clean chicken and cut into 8 pieces (2 each of legs, thighs, wings, and breasts).
2. Season with salt and let stand for 30 minutes.
3. Place chicken and celery in pot and add boiling water.
4. Cook slowly, approximately 1 hour or until chicken is tender.
5. Add rice and cook 30 minutes longer, or until rice is tender.

Rice Pudding

Yield: 6 servings

INGREDIENTS NEEDED
½ c white rice
1 qt milk
½ tsp cinnamon or nutmeg
½ c sugar (brown or white)
½ tsp salt
2 eggs
½ c raisins

EQUIPMENT NEEDED
Liquid and dry measures
Shallow hotel pan
Colander
Wire whip
Oven, preheated to 325°F

PROCEDURE

1. Wash rice.
2. Add remaining ingredients, except for eggs and raisins, and pour into greased hotel pan.
3. Bake for 1 hour in 325°F oven.
4. Stir frequently during first hour of baking.
5. Beat eggs with wire whip.
6. Add eggs and raisins during last half hour of baking.
7. Baking time may vary depending on rice.

Rice Jambalaya

Yield: 8 servings

INGREDIENTS NEEDED
¼ c butter or margarine
1 c white rice
2 oz mushrooms, chopped
½ c onion, chopped
½ c green pepper, chopped
½ c celery, diced fine
3 c beef broth or water
2 c stewed tomatoes
½ tsp chili powder
2 tsp salt

EQUIPMENT NEEDED
Cutting board
French knife
Sauté pan
Shallow hotel pan
Aluminum foil
Oven, preheated to 350°F

PROCEDURE

1. Melt butter or margarine in sauté pan.
2. Add rice and cook, stirring constantly, for about 10 minutes or until it is browned.
3. Add mushrooms, onion, green pepper, and celery.
4. Cook until vegetables are tender.
5. Stir in remaining ingredients.
6. Place in greased hotel pan and cover with aluminum foil.
7. Bake at 350°F for 45 minutes.
8. Remove cover and bake for 10 minutes longer.

Fried Rice

Yield: 8 servings

INGREDIENTS NEEDED
1⅓ c uncooked rice
4 tbsp shortening (Crisco)
2 c cooked popcorn shrimp
1 large onion, diced medium
2 eggs, slightly beaten
½ tsp salt
1 tsp monosodium glutamate
4 tsp soy sauce
2 green onions, chopped
½ c shredded lettuce

EQUIPMENT NEEDED
Cutting board
French knife
Liquid and dry measures
Large, heavy frying pan

PROCEDURE

1. Prepare rice using range-top method. (Yield should be approx. 4 c.) Let cool.
2. Melt shortening in frying pan.
3. Add the shrimp and onion and cook until golden brown.
4. Add eggs, rice, salt, monosodium glutamate, soy sauce, green onion, and lettuce, and cook until lettuce is wilted.

Broccoli-Rice Bake

Yield: 6 servings

INGREDIENTS NEEDED
½ c celery, chopped fine
½ c onion, chopped fine
½ c margarine
1 can cream of mushroom soup
½ c water
8 oz melted cheddar cheese
10 oz fresh broccoli, steamed
7-oz package precooked rice

EQUIPMENT NEEDED
Cutting board
French knife
Liquid and dry measures
Can opener
Sauté pan
Shallow hotel pan
Oven, preheated to 350°F

PROCEDURE

1. Cook celery and onion in melted margarine until golden brown.
2. Combine soup, water, and cheese.
3. Chop and steam broccoli until tender.
4. Cook rice according to package directions.
5. Combine all ingredients.
6. Place in greased hotel pan.
7. Bake at 350°F for 45 minutes.

PRODUCT EVALUATION SHEET

Name _____ Lab date _____

Product prepared_____ Total prep time _____

Cooking method_____

Describe the following in one or two short sentences.

APPEARANCE (size, shape, consistency, etc.):

COLOR (golden brown, pasty white, bright, dull, etc.):

TEXTURE (smooth, lumpy, fine, coarse, sticky, gummy, etc.):

FLAVOR (sweet, sour, bitter, strong, spicy, bland, etc.):

TEMPERATURE (warm, hot, cold . . . Is it appropriate for the product?):

PROBLEMS ENCOUNTERED:

SOLUTION:
Suggestions to alter or improve the product:
1.

2.

Rating (10 being perfect):

0   1   2   3   4   5   6   7   8   9   10

14

Pasta

Pasta is a mild-flavored flour-and-water product that was probably developed when people had to find uses for foodstuffs they had on hand. Usually, vegetable purees and other flavors such as curry or sesame are added as well.

Western pasta is made with water and a hard durum winter wheat flour, which is rich in gluten and "stronger" than ordinary flour. **Semolina** is fine pasta flour milled from durum wheat. One of the coarser grinds of this wheat, it makes pasta that stays whole in boiling water and lends itself to diverse shapes.

Preparing Fresh Pasta

Facilities

Be sure that you have plenty of work space. Use a counter or table that is the right height for you to mix and knead the dough. Avoid plastic or laminated surfaces—the dough will stick to them. Keep the work surface clean by scraping off bits of sticky dough, and keep it lightly floured.

To store your pasta while it is drying out and resting, empty a counter and cover it with clean, lightly floured kitchen towels. Leave room to set out the rolled-out dough and the finished, cut pasta.

Equipment

To prepare the dough you need a fork, measuring cups, and spoons. Mix the dough in a large stainless steel bowl or directly on the counter or table top. To roll out the dough, use either a rolling pin or a pasta machine. The rolling pins used in Italy are long, thin ones (sold in this country as "French" rolling pins!). A long pin will roll out more dough, but a regular rolling pin will also do very well.

Use the machine or a sharp knife to cut the rolled-out dough into noodle strips. Dry out the ready noodles by placing them on the kitchen towels, as described above.

It takes a very large kettle to cook pasta. Because you will have to fill it with water and lift it, choose a kettle that is not very heavy in itself. To drain the pasta use a colander or a spoon-shaped pasta rake.

How Much Dry Pasta to Cook

Macaroni and spaghetti approximately double in volume while cooking; egg noodles remain about the same. When a pasta product is used for the main dish, allow 2 ounces of uncooked product per person. However, consider the appetites of your "market": In some places, 4 ounces of pasta is the appropriate amount for one serving.

Let the chart in Figure 14-1 guide you in determining quantities when one type of pasta is substituted for another and in deciding how

PRODUCT	DRY	COOKED
Elbow macaroni	2 c (8 oz)	4½ c (approx.)
Spaghetti	8 oz	5 c (approx.)
Egg noodles	8 oz (about 4 c)	4 c (approx.)

FIGURE 14-1   Quantity Guide for Pasta

much to prepare for a given number of persons. Eight ounces of uncooked product will usually yield about four servings.

Mass Production of Pasta

The modern pasta plant is almost completely automated. Semolina, farina, or other high-quality hard wheat flour is purchased in bulk and arrives by rail in airslide cars. A pneumatic unloading system transfers it to bulk storage bins, which automatically stop loading when they are full. A second pneumatic transfer system moves the flour to press bins for mixing with water.

The dough is kneaded, then forced by presses through dies (metal discs with holes). Dies are available for making at least 325 shapes of pasta!

The size and shape of the die holes determine what the finished product will be. Round or oval holes, varying from ⅛ to 5/64 of an inch, produce the solid rods that are fedelini, linguine, and other forms of spaghetti. When steel pins are placed in the holes of the die, the extruded dough is tubular and is called macaroni. If the pin has a notch on one side, the dough passes more quickly through one side of the hole than the other. The result is a slightly curved product, such as the familiar elbow macaroni. A revolving knife attached to the die cuts the dough at frequent intervals into short lengths. For even more variety, the extruded dough can be cut into different lengths.

Drying is the most critical step in the manufacture of pasta. The pasta is automatically conveyed to drying units. Longer products, such as spaghetti and long macaroni, are hung on rods. Elbow macaroni, other short goods, and special shapes are spread on belts. The products are dropped from level to level; at each level the moisture is reduced.

Usually a product goes through a preliminary dryer and a finishing dryer. The air temperature and moisture and the length of time in the dryer must be determined accurately for each product. If drying is too fast, the pasta will crack and break easily; if drying is too slow, the product can spoil.

Egg noodles are mixed in much the same way as macaroni and spaghetti, but with the addition of 5.5 percent egg solids (fresh, powdered, or frozen) as required by law. The dough is pressed between rollers. This forms thin sheets, which are then cut to desired widths. The drying procedure is similar to that for other pasta products.

Basic Egg Pasta

Yield: 1 ½ pounds

INGREDIENTS NEEDED
4 large eggs
½ c water
4 tsp oil, preferably olive
3 c all-purpose flour
½ tsp salt
1 c all-purpose flour (for kneading, rolling, and cutting)

EQUIPMENT NEEDED
Liquid and dry measures
Large stainless steel bowl
Rolling pin
French knife
Towels
Fork
Spoons
Wire whip

PROCEDURE

1. In large bowl beat eggs, water, and oil with wire whip until well mixed. Add flour and salt.
2. Using circular motion, continue to mix until egg and flour mixtures are well combined, scraping sides of bowl with fork occasionally.
3. Gather dough together using fork, hands, or spatula.
4. Sprinkle work surface with some of flour reserved for kneading, rolling, and cutting. Turn dough out onto floured surface and sprinkle lightly with more flour.
5. Knead until dough is no longer sticky and a smooth elastic ball is formed (about 5 minutes). The dough should have a firm bounce and a velvety feel. Gently rub all sides of dough lightly with flour.
6. Cover dough with a bowl, and let it rest at room temperature 15 minutes.
7. Cut into four equal portions.
8. Form one portion of dough into a ball. On a lightly floured surface (use some remaining flour reserved for kneading, cutting, and rolling), flatten dough slightly with rolling pin.
9. Roll dough into a circle about 17 to 18 inches in diameter and about the thickness of a dime. As you roll, turn circle frequently, occasionally flouring both bottom and top with enough flour to prevent dough from sticking to surface.
10. Fold dough toward yourself, jelly roll fashion, flouring continuously. Roll should be approximately 16 inches long and 2½ inches thick.
11. Using a French knife, cut roll of dough crosswise into noodles of desired widths.
12. Sprinkle folded noodles lightly with flour; toss very lightly to separate.
13. Hang noodles to dry, or lay out on towels. Cover with a towel.

PRODUCT EVALUATION SHEET

Name _____   Lab date_____

Product prepared_____   Total prep time _____

Cooking method_____

Describe the following in one or two short sentences.

APPEARANCE (size, shape, consistency, etc.):

COLOR (golden brown, pasty white, bright, dull, etc.):

TEXTURE (smooth, lumpy, fine, coarse, sticky, gummy, etc.):

FLAVOR (sweet, sour, bitter, strong, spicy, bland, etc.):

TEMPERATURE (warm, hot, cold . . . Is it appropriate for the product?):

PROBLEMS ENCOUNTERED:

SOLUTION:
Suggestions to alter or improve the product:
1.

2.

Rating (10 being perfect):

0 1 2 3 4 5 6 7 8 9 10

15

Fish and Seafood

Kinds of Fish

About 200 different varieties of fish and seafood are sold in our markets today. Most come from the oceans; some are from lakes and rivers. They are classified into two general groups: finfish and shellfish. The **finfish** come from both salt and fresh water and have scales and fins. Some **shellfish,** including oysters, clams, and scallops, are enclosed in hard shells. Others, such as lobster, crab, and shrimp, have crustlike shells and segmented bodies.

Fish are also classified as **lean** or **fatty** according to the amount of fat they contain. (In any case, fish contains much less fat than red meat.) The flesh of fish with a higher fat content is yellow, pink, or grayish in color, whereas white fish is less fatty. Fatty fish include salmon, mackerel, and tuna; the leaner varieties include haddock, cod, and halibut. Most shellfish contain little fat and are lean.

Market Forms

Fish and seafood are available in several forms: fresh, frozen, canned, dried, smoked, and pickled. About half the fish used in the United States is fresh or frozen, and the remainder is canned. Only a small amount of cured fish is used in our country, but it is very popular in Scandinavia. The many available kinds of fresh, frozen, canned, and cured fish can add variety and interest to your entrees.

Fresh Fish

Following are the five most common forms of fresh fish:

Whole fish. Fish marketed just as it comes from the water; also known as **round** fish. The scales and entrails (the internal organs) must be removed before cooking.

Drawn fish. Fish with only the entrails removed. The head, fins, and scales remain on the fish.

Dressed fish. Fish ready for cooking. The head, tail, fins, scales, and entrails are removed.

Steaks. Cross-sectioned slices of dressed fish. Large fish such as halibut and salmon are often sold as steaks. The backbone is usually the only bone in a fish steak.

Fillets. A lengthwise cut away from the backbone (see Fig. 15-1). A single fillet comes from one side of the fish; a double or butterfly fillet comes from both sides of the fish and is held together by uncut flesh and skin. You will find only a few (sometimes no) bones in a fillet. The market forms of fresh fish are illustrated in Figure 15-2.

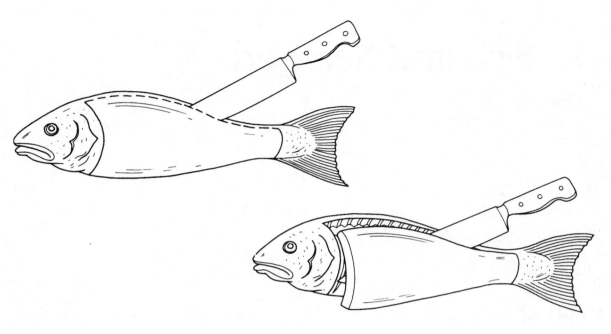

FIGURE 15-1   Filleting Fish

Frozen Fish

Several varieties of frozen fish are available year-round. Purchased frozen fish can be even fresher than fresh fish because much of the freezing takes place directly on the fishing boats. Frozen fish is usually sold in fillets and steaks. **Fish sticks,** which are cut from fillets, may be breaded and partially cooked before freezing. Breaded, uncooked fillets and shellfish are also sold frozen.

Canned Fish

Both finfish and shellfish are canned in a variety of forms. Popular canned finfish include salmon, tuna, and sardines. Varieties of canned shellfish—often considered a delicacy—include oysters, clams, lobsters, crab, scallops, and shrimp.

Cured Fish

Fish that has been salted, smoked, or pickled is referred to as **cured fish.** Curing preserves fish and also gives it a distinctive flavor. Mildly salted fish is sometimes treated with smoke, which imparts a special smoky taste.

Examples of cured fish are salt cod, mackerel, finnan haddie, kippered herring, and anchovies. Cod or herring is salted in dry salt or brine and then dried. Finnan haddie is haddock that has been cured in brine and then smoked. Kippers, salmon, and whitefish may also be cured. Pickled fish is cured in a brine that contains vinegar and spices and, after processing, is packed into jars.

Selection of Fish

Unlike meat inspection, inspection and grading of fish for wholesomeness is voluntary. Because inspection is not mandatory, it is important to purchase finfish from reliable sources.

Some of the fish products that you may buy may bear stamps indicating that they have been inspected. The voluntary grading program is supervised by the United States Department of the Interior. The grading standards usually classify fish as U.S. Grade A, U.S. Grade B, and substandard. When available, this grading will enable you to purchase a wholesome, good quality, fresh product.

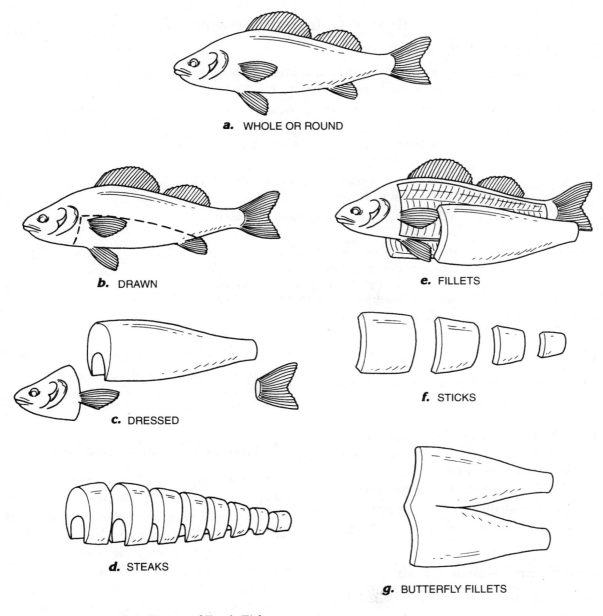

a. WHOLE OR ROUND

b. DRAWN

e. FILLETS

c. DRESSED

f. STICKS

d. STEAKS

g. BUTTERFLY FILLETS

FIGURE 15-2   Market Forms of Fresh Fish

Shellfish

Shellfish is sold live in the shell, shucked (shell removed), and cooked. The following characteristics are clues to the freshness of shellfish:

1. Shucked oysters and clams are plump and creamy in color. The liquid they are in is odorless and clear.

2. Shells of live clams and oysters should be tightly closed or should close when touched.

3. The tail of a live lobster snaps back quickly after it is flattened out. (Both lobster and crab should be kept alive until they are cooked.)

4. The fresh deep-sea scallop is white; the bay scallop is creamy white or pinkish.

5. Shrimp should be odorless, and the thin shell covering them should be firmly attached.

BUYING GUIDE FOR FINFISH

MARKET FORM	DESCRIPTION	SERVING AMOUNT
Whole or round	As it comes from the water. Must be scaled, cleaned; head, tail, fins must be removed.	1 pound
Drawn	Cleaned only. Scales, head, tail, fins must be removed.	1 pound
Dressed	Scaled and cleaned, usually with head, tail, fins removed. Ready for cooking.	½ pound
Steaks	Cross-section slices of large dressed fish, with a section of the backbone.	⅓ pound
Fillets	Side of fish, cut lengthwise from the backbone; boneless.	½ pound
Sticks	Pieces of fish cut from blocks of frozen fillets into portions of uniform dimensions, usually 1-ounce portions. Usually covered with batter, breaded and browned in deep fat or baked.	3 1-ounce sticks per serving

Finfish

Here are several characteristics that will help you judge the freshness of finfish:

1. The whole or round fish should have bulging, bright, clear eyes; bright red gills; and scales that cling to the skin.
2. The flesh should be firm and springy and hold no indentation when pressed.
3. There should be no disagreeable odor.

Frozen and Canned Fish

Choose only fish that is solidly frozen, in packages that show no signs of being thawed and refrozen. Like fresh fish, some frozen and processed fish may not have a government grade. The information on the label and the brand name are your only clues to quality.

Amount of Fish to Buy

The amount you buy is determined by the form of fish. Canned and frozen fish are ready for cooking and therefore will have no waste. Fresh whole or drawn fish will have waste. There is less waste in dressed fish because the entrails, head, tail, fins, and scales have been removed. Fish

steaks will have little waste, and fillets of finfish will have no waste. The tables on pages 82 and 83 will help you determine how much fish to buy.

Methods of Fish Cookery

Seafood can be baked, boiled, broiled, deep-fried, sautéed, panfried, poached, or steamed. The type of fish or seafood and its market form dictate the best cooking method. Seafood is best cooked by dry methods if fatty and with moist heat if lean. Fatty fish, such as salmon, trout, mackerel, or shad, can be baked, broiled, or fried. Lean fish, such as sole or cod, is best steamed, boiled, simmered, poached, or prepared to be served with a moist sauce. See the glossary at the end of the chapter for definitions of terms used in fish cookery.

Baking

Baking means placing fish into dry heat to cook. Whole fish, parts, or slices can be baked. Preheat the oven to 350°F, and bake fish only until done. Overcooking dries the fish out and produces a poor product.

Some fish are fat enough to bake well without any extra preparation. Other fish must be

BUYING GUIDE FOR SHELLFISH

MARKET FORM	ITEM	SERVING AMOUNT
Live	Clams, oysters	6
	Crabs	3
	Lobster	1 pound
Shucked	Oysters, clams	⅓ pint
	Scallops	⅓ pound
Fresh or frozen	Shrimp	¼ pound
	Lobster tails	½ pound
Cooked in the shell	Crabs	3
	Lobster	1 pound
Cooked, shelled	Shrimp, crab, lobster	¼ pound

barded (strips of fat pork or meat laid over the product) to add moistness. Some fish are basted during baking so they stay moist; others may be baked in a sauce.

Fish can be baked from the frozen state, provided the cooking time is increased to allow for thawing during the cooking process and the fish does not need special handling such as stuffing before being baked.

Most chefs consider baking to be a poor method of preparation. Few shellfish are baked.

Boiling

Boiling means adding seafood to boiling, salted, seasoned water and cooking gently until the product is done. Use only a simmering temperature to help prevent delicate products from breaking up. Cook only to doneness. Fish that might break up is cooked on a trivet so it can be lifted up easily without breaking apart.

A fish that is to be decorated when cold is prepared in the same manner and then is allowed to chill thoroughly before being handled. Chilling makes the fish firm.

Cooking for too long or at too high a temperature toughens the proteins, especially in shellfish. Clams and oysters become very tough when overcooked. An overboiled lobster also can be very tough. Fish and shellfish frequently are cooked in court bouillon, a seasoned stock that adds flavor to the product.

Broiling

Broiling is a dry-heat method that uses radiated heat. Thin products dry out easily when broiled, so fish to be cooked this way should be large enough to handle well. Fatty fish broil well; lean fish do not.

To broil cod or sole, first dip the product into flour and then into oil, and then baste with oil during broiling. Even with this method, cod or sole is not as good as the more fatty varieties when broiled.

Frozen fish is usually thawed before being broiled. Be sure to follow the manufacturer's direction for operating the broiler and cooking specific seafood items. Broiling time depends on the thickness of the item, the type of product, and the distance from the heat.

As in other preparation methods, all seafood should be broiled only as much as is needed. A general guide is to place the fish 3 to 4 inches from the heat source (thicker cuts farther away than thinner ones) and broil for 10 to 15 minutes. Thicker pieces, such as pan-dressed fish, may have to be turned several times. Do not pierce fish with a fork; roll it over. Some fish may have to be broiled in a double grid, which encloses the fish and allows it to be turned without breaking. Broiling fish can be basted with fat or a sauce.

Lobsters can be broiled successfully. Split the lobsters and place them 4 inches from the heat source for 12 to 15 minutes. Broiled seafood should be served very hot. A maître d'hôtel butter or meunière butter can be served with broiled fish, or it can be garnished with a lemon wedge.

Deep-Frying

Deep-frying is immersion in hot oil. Deep-frying cooks many seafoods well, especially if they have been breaded or dipped in batter to stay moist. The best frying temperature is 350°F.

Pieces of uniform size should be cooked together. Fry only one layer of fish at a time, allowing enough room so pieces do not touch in the frying basket. Overloading the basket will drop oil temperature and result in a grease-soaked product. The fish should be fried until it is golden brown, flakes easily, and is cooked throughout. In most cases the fish will rise to the top of the fat and "swim." Frozen seafoods usually must be thawed before frying, although small pieces such as breaded shrimp, scallops, and fish sticks can be fried while frozen.

After frying, drain the fish immediately on absorbent paper to remove excess fat. Keep the product warm under an infrared lamp or in a dry, warm place. Holding too long results in a poorer product.

Panfrying or Sautéing

Panfrying and **sautéing** are range-top methods. Panfried or sautéed fish is a common menu item because fish responds well to this cooking method. Slightly more fat is used for panfrying than for sautéing.

These methods are excellent for dressed fish, fillets, or steaks. The products can be plain, floured, or breaded. Batter-dipped products usually are not panfried. The product is sautéed until brown on both sides. The fish may have to be turned several times. About 8 to 10 minutes of frying time is needed, depending on the thickness of the fish.

Poaching

Poaching entails placing the product in a single layer in a shallow pan, barely covered with liquid. Fish may be poached in plain water with seasonings; in water with wine, milk, tomato juice, or other liquids; or in court bouillon. The liquid, if properly prepared, will contribute additional seasoning to the fish. Cloves, bay leaves, crushed peppercorns, and a few other herbs or spices are added to the poaching water. The juice of a lemon and sliced or twisted rind can also be added. For the best results, simmer 5 to 10 minutes because the flesh of many seafoods is very delicate.

Leftover fish can be poached and flaked to make excellent casseroles, salads, and appetizers. Again, to prevent the food from breaking up, place a trivet under the fish, or wrap it in cheesecloth.

Cod, flounder, haddock, halibut, ocean perch, pompano, salmon, sea bass, sole, and other lean, white-fleshed fish are best for poaching. Poached fish can be served simply, with lemon butter or other butters, or with a sauce such as hollandaise.

Steaming

In **steaming,** seafood is cooked over a court bouillon. Fish that poach well also steam well. Seafood usually should be steamed in a perforated pan. The flavors of a court bouillon stock rise and add flavor to the steamed fish. Steaming in a pressure cooker can result in a toughened, unpalatable product if the fish is cooked too long. The fish is done when the flesh loses its translucent appearance and becomes opaque. A fork placed in the thickest part of the flesh should be able to flake the fish apart.

Handling and Storage

Fish and shellfish are some of the most perishable foods you will handle. It is especially important to store them carefully and use them quickly. The "fishy" taste that turns many people away from fish is actually a sign of decompo-

---

CHECKLIST FOR FRESHNESS

CHARACTERISTICS	FRESH FISH	NOT-SO-FRESH FISH
Odor	Fresh and mild, no off odors	Strong, "fishy" odor
Eyes	Clear, shiny, bulging	Cloudy, sunken
Gills	Red or pink	Grey or brown
Texture of flesh	Firm, elastic	Soft, easily dented
Scales	Shiny, tight on skin	Loose, not shiny

---

sition. Fresh fish should taste and smell sweet and fresh. Remember—because fresh fish is not federally inspected, it is up to you to check for quality.

Fresh Fish

In storing fresh fish, you will have four objectives:

1. To prevent spoilage or decomposition
2. To keep the fish moist
3. To prevent fish odors and flavors from being transferred to other foods
4. To protect the delicate flesh from being bruised or crushed

Fish should be stored at a temperature of 30°F to 34°F. **Crushed ice** is the preferred storage method. Use drip pans to allow for drainage of melted ice. Change ice at least twice per day. Cover the container or store it in a separate box, away from other foods. A **refrigerated box** may be used if crushed ice storage is not available or practical. Wrap all fish, or leave it in the original moistureproof wrap.

Fresh fish may be stored for 1 or 2 days. If it must be kept longer, you may (1) wrap and freeze it immediately or (2) cook and then refrigerate it for later use in recipes calling for cooked fish.

Check stored fish for freshness just before you use it. Even if it was fresh when received, it may not be fresh after a few days in storage. The following checklist provides guidelines. However, because most fish is purchased not whole or dressed but as fillets, steaks, or other portions, odor is a primary check for freshness.

Frozen Fish

Frozen products account for more of the fish served today than do fresh products. If it were not for the wide availability of frozen seafood, commercial kitchens would serve much less of it than they do.

Checking the quality of frozen seafood is essential to preparing and serving wholesome, palatable products. Follow these guidelines:

1. Make sure that frozen products are frozen when received, not thawed.
2. Look for a fresh, sweet odor or no odor at all. Strong, "fishy" odor means poor handling.
3. Make sure that items are well wrapped, with no freezer burn.
4. Some frozen fish is glazed with a thin layer of ice to prevent drying. Check for a shiny surface to make sure the glaze has not melted off or evaporated.

You can preserve quality by implementing proper storage procedures:

1. Store frozen seafood at 0°F or colder.
2. Keep products well wrapped to prevent freezer burn.
3. Observe the maximum storage times: 2 months for fatty fish, 6 months for lean fish.
4. Rotate stock—first in, first out.

SEAFOOD COOKING TERMS

Baste: To moisten foods with liquid or fat during the cooking process

Bread: To coat by dipping in flour, egg wash, and bread crumbs

Court bouillon: A stock in or over which fish is cooked; made from water, vegetables, vinegar or wine, and herbs and spices

Delicate: Tender and likely to break easily

Fillets: The sides of a fish, cut lengthwise along the backbone

Fish: Water animals that have fins

Meunière: A sauce made with butter, lemon juice, and parsley

Opaque: Not able to be seen through

Parchment: A waterproof, grease-resistant paper

Poach: To simmer in court bouillon

Sauté: To cook lightly in a small amount of butter or oil

Shellfish: Water animals that have shells

Smelt: A very small fish that is usually panfried

Steaks: Cross-sections of fairly large fish

Translucent: Able to be seen through

Procedures for thawing and handling frozen fish will vary with the market form and the style of preparation. Small pieces (fillets, steaks, portions) up to 8 ounces can be cooked from the frozen state. This makes handling easier and prevents excessive drip loss. Large fish should be thawed for more even cooking from surface to interior.

Thaw frozen raw fish in the cooler, never at room temperature. Allow 18 to 36 hours, depending on size. Alternatively, if pressed for time, keep the fish in the original moistureproof wrapper and thaw under cold running water.

Fillets or other portions that are to be breaded or prepared in some other way before cooking may be partially thawed (for example, for a few seconds in a microwave oven), then prepped and cooked. They will handle more easily than if fully thawed.

Handle thawed fish as you would fresh fish. Do not refreeze.

Stuffed Baked Fish

Yield: About 8 servings

INGREDIENTS NEEDED

1 dressed trout (4 to 5 lb)
⅓ c butter or margarine
2 medium onions, chopped fine
3 stalks celery, chopped
3 apples, cored and chopped
1 tbsp parsley, chopped fine
1 c mushrooms, sliced
4 c dry bread cubes
2 tsp sugar
½ tsp thyme
2 tsp lemon juice
3 eggs, lightly beaten
1 c white wine
Salt and pepper

EQUIPMENT NEEDED

Cutting board
French knife
Apple corer
Liquid and dry measures
Sauté pan
Small roasting pan
Skewers (metal or wood)
Pastry brush
Oven, preheated to 350°F

PROCEDURE

1. Sprinkle cavity of fish with salt and pepper.
2. For stuffing, melt ⅛ cup butter or margarine in sauté pan. Add onion and celery. Stir-fry until onion is transparent. Add apples, parsley, and mushrooms. Stir-fry 2 minutes longer.
3. Mixed cooked vegetables with bread cubes, sugar, thyme, lemon juice, eggs, and wine. Blend well.
4. Fill fish cavity with stuffing. Close cavity with skewers. Place fish in roasting pan, and drizzle with melted butter.
5. Bake at 350°F about 40 minutes or until fish flakes easily. Baste occasionally with additional melted butter.

Seafood Kabobs

Yield: 6 servings

INGREDIENTS NEEDED

1 lobster tail, 8 oz, cut in 6 pieces
6 scallops
6 shrimp, peeled and deveined
12 large mushroom caps
½ c olive oil
3 tbsp soy sauce
1 tbsp Worcestershire sauce
2 tbsp white wine
2 tbsp wine vinegar
½ tbsp lemon juice
½ tsp lemon peel
½ tsp ground pepper
2 tsp snipped parsley
18 (4-in.) pieces sliced bacon
12 (1-in.) squares green pepper
6 cherry tomatoes

EQUIPMENT NEEDED

Cutting board
French knife
Liquid and dry measures
Shallow hotel pan
Broiler
Skewers, wood or metal (10-in.)
Pastry brush
Blender

PROCEDURE

1. Put lobster pieces, scallops, shrimp, and mushroom caps into hotel pan.
2. Combine olive oil, soy sauce, Worcestershire sauce, wine, vinegar, lemon peel, lemon juice, pepper, and parsley in blender and mix vigorously. Pour the marinade over seafood and mushroom caps, and set aside for 1 hour.
3. Drain off marinade and reserve.
4. Wrap each piece of seafood in bacon. Thread pieces on skewers as follows: green pepper, lobster, mushroom, scallop, mushroom, shrimp, and green pepper. Arrange on a broiler and brush with marinade.
5. Place under broiler 3 inches from heat. Broil 10 to 12 minutes, turning and brushing frequently with marinade. Add a cherry tomato to each skewer during last few minutes of broiling.

Stir-Fried Shrimp and Vegetables

Yield: 4 servings

INGREDIENTS NEEDED

¼ lb fresh bean sprouts
2 tbsp cornstarch
2 tsp sugar
1½ c water
2 tbsp soy sauce
3 tbsp wine vinegar
½ tsp pepper
3 tbsp vegetable oil
1 tsp salt
1 c celery, sliced diagonally
6 green onions, sliced diagonally
1 c mushrooms, sliced thin
2 cloves garlic, minced
1 tsp ginger root, minced
¾ lb cleaned, cooked shrimp
6 oz snow peas
4 c cooked white rice

EQUIPMENT NEEDED

Cutting board
French knife
Liquid and dry measures
Large sauté pan or wok
Small saucepan
China cap
Wooden spoon
Paper towels

PROCEDURE

1. Blanch bean sprouts by turning half of them into china cap and setting in saucepan of boiling water. Boil 1 minute. Remove from water and spread out on absorbent paper to drain. Repeat with remaining bean sprouts.

2. Blend cornstarch, sugar, water, soy sauce, vinegar, and pepper; set aside.

3. Heat 2 tablespoons vegetable oil in large sauté pan. Stir in salt, celery, green onions, and mushrooms. Stir-fry vegetables about 1 minute. Add bean sprouts and stir-fry 1 minute more. Remove vegetables from sauté pan.

4. Heat 1 tablespoon vegetable oil. Add garlic and ginger root; stir-fry briefly. Add shrimp and snow peas; stir-fry 2 minutes longer. Return other vegetables to sauté pan and mix together. Stir-fry briefly about 2 minutes to heat.

5. Stir cornstarch mixture into liquid in center of large sauté pan or wok. Cook until thickened, and combine with shrimp and vegetables.

6. Serve immediately over cooked white rice.

Veracruz Style Crab-Filled Fish Rolls

Yield: 6 servings

INGREDIENTS NEEDED

6 sole fillets, cut into long, thin slices
Juice of 1 lemon
½ cup milk
2 tbsp vegetable oil
½ c onion, chopped
1 clove garlic, minced
1 small tomato, peeled and chopped
1 tsp parsley, minced
1 tsp salt
Dash of pepper
¼ lb sea legs, shredded
¼ lb Monterey Jack cheese
1 c sour cream
1 egg yolk
¼ lb butter or margarine

EQUIPMENT NEEDED

Cutting board
French knife
Liquid and dry measures
Small sauté pan
Paper towels
Shallow hotel pan
Wire whip
Oven, preheated to 350°F

PROCEDURE

1. Rinse fish; rub with lemon juice; soak in milk.
2. Meanwhile, heat vegetable oil in sauté pan. Sauté onion and garlic in oil; add tomato and cook until no longer juicy. Remove from heat and stir in parsley, salt, and pepper. Add sea legs and one-third of cheese, and mix well.
3. Remove fish from milk and pat dry with paper towels. Place a small amount of sea legs on one end of fillet and roll up, as for a jelly roll. Place fish rolls in one layer in greased hotel pan.
4. Beat sour cream and egg yolk with wire whip, and pour over fish rolls. Dot with butter. Sprinkle remaining cheese over top.
5. Bake at 350°F until product is golden brown and cheese is melted.
6. Serve immediately.

Fish Fillets Florentine

Yield: 6 to 8 servings

INGREDIENTS NEEDED
3 lb fresh spinach
¼ c butter
1½ tbsp flour
½ tsp salt
⅛ tsp pepper
1½ c milk
½ c grated Parmesan cheese
2 lb white fish fillets

EQUIPMENT NEEDED
Cutting board
French knife
Liquid and dry measures
Colander
Shallow hotel pan
Sauté pan
Oven, preheated to 375°F

PROCEDURE

1. Wash spinach thoroughly and cook without adding water.
2. When spinach is barely tender, drain and chop coarsely.
3. Place in hotel pan.
4. Melt butter in sauté pan, and blend in flour and seasonings.
5. Add milk and cook until thickened, stirring constantly.
6. Add cheese and continue heating until cheese has melted.
7. Pour sauce over spinach, place fish fillets on top, and bake at 375°F for 30 minutes.
8. Serve immediately.

Salmon à la King

Yield: 6 servings

INGREDIENTS NEEDED
2 c cooked or canned salmon
½ c butter or margarine, melted
½ c celery, chopped
½ c green pepper, chopped
¼ c flour
½ tsp salt
1½ c milk
8 oz mushrooms, sliced
2 tbsp pimento, chopped
3 c cooked white rice

EQUIPMENT NEEDED
Cutting board
French knife
Liquid and dry measures
Medium-size saucepan
Mixing spoon

PROCEDURE

1. Break salmon into small chunks.
2. Melt butter or margarine in saucepan. Add celery and green pepper, and cook over low heat until vegetables are tender.
3. Gradually add flour and salt, and stir until smooth.
4. Slowly add milk and cook gently, stirring, until sauce is thick and smooth.
5. Add salmon, mushrooms, and pimento.
6. Heat mixture and serve over cooked rice.

PRODUCT EVALUATION SHEET

Name _____ Lab date _____

Product prepared_____ Total prep time _____

Cooking method_____

Describe the following in one or two short sentences.

APPEARANCE (size, shape, consistency, etc.):

COLOR (golden brown, pasty white, bright, dull, etc.):

TEXTURE (smooth, lumpy, fine, coarse, sticky, gummy, etc.):

FLAVOR (sweet, sour, bitter, strong, spicy, bland, etc.):

TEMPERATURE (warm, hot, cold . . . Is it appropriate for the product?):

PROBLEMS ENCOUNTERED:

SOLUTION:
Suggestions to alter or improve the product:
1.

2.

Rating (10 being perfect):

0   1   2   3   4   5   6   7   8   9   10

16

Poultry and Game Birds

Kinds of Poultry

Poultry includes chicken, Cornish hen, turkey, duck, goose, guinea fowl, and squab. Poultry is raised for the table. It is contrasted with **game birds,** which include grouse, pheasant, partridge, quail, peacock, wild duck, and wild turkey.

Chicken is the largest poultry group, with turkeys in a distant second place. Poultry is inexpensive compared to most meats because it is now scientifically mass-produced and is available year-round. In the past, poultry was a seasonal dish: Fresh fryers and roasting chickens appeared on the market only in summer and fall; at other times, they came frozen. Today most of the poultry on the market is fresh. Exceptions are ducks, some turkeys, and geese. The chicken now produced in quantity is a cross between a rock Cornish chicken and a white Plymouth Rock chicken. This bird has a lot of white, delicate meat.

You can ascertain the approximate age of any bird by moving the keel bone on its breastbone. A flexible keel bone indicates that the bone is still gelatinous and thus that the bird is still growing.

Chicken

Chicken is popular all over the world. In many areas it is a dish for special company.

Following are the various classifications of chicken:

Broiler. A young chicken, usually 9 weeks old, of either sex, raised for meat. A tender-meated bird with soft, pliable, smooth skin and flexible breastbone cartilage, it usually weighs from 1½ to 3½ pounds.

Fryer. The same as a broiler, but a slightly larger bird.

Bro-hen. The laying hen of the broiler industry, about 1½ years old, weighing 4½ to 6 pounds and having a high ratio of meat to bone.

Capon. A neutered male chicken, weighing about 4 to 7 pounds, tender and flavorful, with a lot of white meat. These birds are more expensive and do not provide great yield.

Fowl. A mature female averaging 5 to 6 pounds, usually referred to as a **stewing hen.** It is usually marketed when past its ideal age for laying. Fowl is less tender than other poultry and has a higher fat content.

Oven-ready. A term now applied to almost all commercially produced chickens. With pinfeathers removed and hair singed, the bird is thoroughly cleaned inside and out; giblets (edible heart, liver, and gizzard) are cleaned and wrapped and placed in the body cavity. Oven-ready birds are shipped to market in iced wooden crates in refrigerated trucks.

Roaster. A tender chicken weighing 3½ to 5 pounds, now marketed at about 12 weeks of age.

Stag. Usually termed a **rooster.** A stag is tough and stringy and weighs 3 to 6 pounds.

Cornish hen. A small chicken weighing 1 to 2 pounds when mature. High in protein and low in fat, a Cornish hen has a full, chubby breast filled with light, delicate white meat. One bird usually yields one or two servings. Cornish hens are small enough to be prepared and served whole or half. With an attractive garnish, they make a good impression when served.

Turkey

Turkeys are mass-produced on huge turkey farms. As a menu offering, turkey is very competitive with chicken. Many families eat chicken more often than they do turkey because one turkey is a lot for a single family. Thus, when families go out to dine, they often prefer turkey to chicken.

Following are the classifications of turkey:

Fryer-roaster. Turkeys 16 weeks old and weighing about 4 to 8 pounds. They often come from a small breed in which year-old females may weigh only 6 to 10 pounds. A heavy breed used extensively is called the Beltsville, Maryland, by the USDA experimental farms.

Young toms/hens. Young turkeys that range from 12 to 16 pounds for hens and 12 to 30 pounds for toms. Some toms weigh more than 60 pounds, but they are too large for commercial use. Some large birds must be split before roasting because they will not fit in the typical roasting oven.

Yearlings. Turkeys marketed under 15 months of age.

Old toms/hens. Used for picked meat or casserole dishes. They usually are breeding stock.

The carcass or bones of an 18-pound and a 30-pound turkey weigh about the same. Thus it pays to buy the larger bird because the yield is much greater.

Duck

Duck meat is all dark, and the yield is low. The main production area for ducks is Long Island, New York. Ducks are mass-produced in two crops per year, unlike chickens and turkeys, which are in continuous production throughout the year. Therefore, many ducks are marketed frozen.

Ducklings are usually from 7 to 8 weeks old, seldom more than 16 weeks old. The weight range for ducklings is from 3 to 7 pounds; the preferred weight for foodservice is usually from 3½ to 5½ pounds.

Following are the classifications of duck:

Broilers and fryers. Less than 8 weeks old.

Roasters and ducklings. Less than 16 weeks old.

Mature or old ducks. More than 6 months old.

Ducks usually are cut into four quarters, with one portion being a quarter. Foodservice operations seldom use older, tougher birds.

Goose

Geese are generally marketed young because weight gained after the first 11 weeks is mostly in the form of fat. Young geese have tender flesh and weigh from 4 to 10 pounds. Mature or old geese are more than 6 months old and are rarely used in foodservice operations. They usually weigh between 10 and 18 pounds.

Guinea Fowl

Guinea fowl are related to the pheasant family and have a somewhat gamy flavor. The most popular weigh 1 to 1½ pounds. They should be served young because they can be tough.

Squab

Squabs are 3- to 4-week-old pigeons that have never flown; they weigh from 6 to 14 ounces. Producers feed them carefully to produce meat that is tender and light in color. Squab is found only on higher-priced menus because it is a more expensive poultry item.

Market Forms

Fresh-killed poultry is not more than 3 days old, has never been frozen, and has been kept chilled at 27°F to 31°F from time of slaughter to delivery. Most chicken and turkey on the market is fresh killed. **Stored poultry** is more than 3 days old but less than 30 days old. It is not plentiful on the market because the flesh is perishable.

Fresh-frozen poultry has been frozen only a short time and usually is a high-quality product. **Frozen storage poultry** has been in frozen storage longer and may not be as good as the fresh-frozen product. Putting frozen poultry in very tight wraps helps preserve quality. Poultry easily develops freezer burn, a whitish surface dehydration. Once this drying out occurs, the flesh can never be restored to a palatable condition.

Ready-to-cook poultry must be eviscerated, have the heads and feet removed, and the neck and giblets wrapped in parchment paper and placed in the body cavity. The lungs must be removed but not the kidneys.

Poultry is marketed **whole, split, quartered,** and **in parts.** Parts include whole breasts, whole breasts with keel and rib bones removed, regular and boneless half breasts, whole legs, drumsticks, thighs, wings, and backs and necks. Livers, hearts, and gizzards may be sold separately. Some restaurants buy completely deboned and rolled poultry, which is available both fresh and frozen. Rolls should have no more skin than would be normal for the flesh that makes up the rolls.

Cooked poultry meat is also available. It should be sold either (1) in the same ratio of dark to light meat as occurs on the bird or (2) as all white or all dark meat. Skin may or may not be allowed, according to purchase specifications.

The market offers many precooked poultry products, such as à la king, creamed, breaded, tetrazzini, and cacciatore preparations. Many of these items are high quality and are being used in considerable quantities.

Many canned poultry products are available either boned, in pieces, or as whole smaller birds. Other canned poultry items include soups, sandwich spreads, stews, gravies, à la king dishes, creamed dishes with rice or noodles, poultry in gravy, and baby food.

Many foodservice operations purchase their chicken kiev, chicken cordon bleu, boneless legs stuffed with wild rice, and chicken breasts with almond stuffing. These products save labor and present highly merchandisable menu items because they typically are not served in the home.

Grading

Poultry must be inspected and passed for wholesomeness before being shipped. The birds must be processed under rigid sanitary conditions, must contain no harmful chemicals or additives, must be properly processed and packaged, and must be truthfully and informatively labeled.

Grading is mandatory; grades are A, B, and C. The highest, Grade A, denotes good overall shape and appearance and birds that are meaty and practically free from defects. Foodservice operations usually specify Grade A.

Buyers can determine quality by checking for the following:
▼ Confirmation (rounded, full, plump shape)
▼ Fleshing (full)
▼ Fat cover (even distribution of fat)
▼ Skin condition (unblemished, practically free from pinfeathers)

The breastbone should yield to light pressure.

Product and Portion Size

All birds purchased should be of uniform size so that those cooked together are of the same doneness. Uniformity in size also is important in portion control: Serving and merchandising different portion sizes to different customers does not promote good guest relations.

With chicken, the average portion allowance is 8 to 9½ ounces raw weight, or one-quarter of a 2¼- to 2½-pound bird. (This does not include the weight of necks and giblets of ready-to-cook birds.) Chicken breast is best obtained from 2½-pound broilers if only half a breast is used per portion. If a portion is the whole breast, then the smaller broiler is desirable. A breast just removed from the breastbone (without the wing but containing wishbone and skin) will weigh about 5.6 ounces; if the wishbone is removed, it will weigh around 5 ounces.

Methods of Poultry Cookery

Poultry yield depends on the bird's size and fleshing and on the cooking method. Of course, the larger the bird, the greater the yield.

Poultry is cooked by the same methods as meat. Low-temperature cooking (250°F to 325°F) results in less shrinkage and a moister, better-looking product. Poultry is usually considered done when the temperature is 180°F in the thigh or breast center. The meat should feel soft on the thigh, breast, or leg, and the wing should move easily. You can insert a fork into the shoulder muscle of the wing to see if it twists out easily.

Most poultry is cooked well done, except for a few varieties such as duck. Small birds, including squab, are best cooked at higher temperatures (around 400°F) to speed cooking and reduce drying out. Older birds should be cooked in moist heat, younger ones in dry heat.

Barbecuing

Poultry can be barbecued on a grill, over hot coals, or in an oven. Chicken is a popular barbecue item, and turkey and other birds also can be barbecued. Times and temperatures are similar to those for other dry-heat cooking methods. Poultry should be cooked at least 6 inches from the heat. Thick parts or those basted with a sauce high in sugar should be placed 10 inches or more from the heat.

Split, quartered, and cut up pieces are first barbecued skin up so the excess fat can baste them. They then are turned and cooked on the other side. You may want to place some poultry parts in a double grid so they will be easier to turn.

Braising

Fricasseed or stewed poultry may be braised; the braising method is the same as for meat. Tougher birds often are cooked this way, and many tender birds also respond well to this treatment. Chicken cacciatore is a bird braised in a tomato sauce with onions, garlic, herbs, and wine.

Broiling

Chicken commonly is broiled. Pieces are made as flat as possible for an even cooking surface. The wing is folded, tip back, under the side so the thickest part around the shoulder joint is bared. On the drumstick quarter, the leg is turned at right angles to the rest of the body and forced inward; this moves the thigh portion to the inside cavity behind the last rib bone.

Before broiling, chicken and turkey can be dipped into a mixture of cooking oil, paprika, salt, and pepper. Allow 1½ tablespoons paprika, 1 teaspoon white pepper, and 1 tablespoon salt per cup of oil.

Poultry is broiled from 5 to 10 inches from the heat source, depending on the thickness of the part and its fat content. Parts can be broiled just until browned, then placed in pans and finished in a moderate oven. Doneness can be checked by movement of the joints.

Frying

Poultry can be fried in shallow or deep fat. Panfrying or sautéing is done in about ¼ inch of fat at 325°F. Raw poultry should be deep-fried at 325°F; precooked poultry should be cooked at 350°F.

Poultry can be lightly floured or breaded before frying. Some poultry can be dipped in batter and sautéed. For deep-frying, chicken can be dredged with seasoned flour, breaded, or batter dipped. Flour-dredged and breaded birds can be placed in baskets and lowered into the cooking fat. Batter-dipped products should be placed in baskets that have already been lowered into the fat. When deep-frying is completed, the baskets should be lifted and shaken to remove excess fat but not shaken hard enough to break any coating.

A flour coating should amount to 5 percent of the product. Breading should be 10 to 15 percent, and batter 20 percent. Heavy dredging or coating results in a poor product.

Roasting

Smaller birds may have to be trussed before roasting; for larger birds this is usually not necessary. Brush fat on the inside and out, and add seasonings. Paprika will promote browning. Pans should be full, but the birds should not touch one another.

Place large birds breast down on perforated trivets so that the fat from the back bastes the breast as the bird roasts. Small birds can be basted; covered with bacon, salt pork, or other fatty tissues; or covered with oil-soaked cloth. Fat birds such as ducks and geese are roasted breast side up and do not need to be basted. Some chefs presteam ducks and geese to rid them of fat and then finish them by roasting.

The following chart shows times for roasting poultry in a 325°F oven. Larger birds may be roasted more effectively at slightly lower temperatures.

Poaching

In comparison to roasting, poaching gives a greater yield plus more moistness, flavor, and tenderness, especially with large birds. Poaching takes about half as long as roasting and requires less cooking space. More attractive and uniform portions are obtained. If poached boned, much poultry meat can be cut on a slicer.

To prepare a large bird for poaching, section and bone it, or leave the bone in. You can use the bony parts for stock, then pick the cooked meat for use in made-up dishes and salads. The

ROASTING TIMES

READY-TO-COOK WEIGHT IN POUNDS	APPROX. MINUTES PER POUND	TOTAL TIME (HOURS)
1⅓ to 2½	30 to 40	1 to 1¾
2½ to 3½	30 to 40	1½ to 2½
3½ to 4¾	30 to 40	2 to 3
4¾ to 6	30 to 40	3 to 3½
READY-TO-COOK WEIGHT IN POUNDS	APPROX. MINUTES PER POUND	TOTAL TIME (HOURS)
6 to 8	30 to 40	3½ to 4
8 to 10	25 to 30	3 to 3½
10 to 14*	18 to 20	3½ to 4
14 to 18*	15 to 18	4 to 4½
20 to 30*	12 to 15	5 to 6

*unstuffed

sections to be poached should be arranged skin side up in a stockpot, roasting pan, or steam-jacketed kettle. Cover sections with hot water or stock, seasoned with 1 tablespoon salt and 1 teaspoon white pepper for every 6 pounds of bird. The meat is simmered about 2 to 2½ hours or until fork-tender. It is cooled in the stock or plunged into cold water. After reaching room temperature, it is refrigerated at about 40°F. **Use poached meat within 3 days.**

Poach-roasting is a related method for preparing sectioned chickens. Place the parts skin side down in shallow pans. Then cover them about two-thirds of the way with hot stock or seasoned water, and roast in an oven at 350°F. The product comes out as if poached, but it is lightly roasted on the parts that project out of the cooking liquid.

Steaming

Older birds may be cooked by steam pressure. This tenderizes the meat so it can be picked for various uses. In high-pressure steamers (15 psi), chicken legs, thighs, and wings cook tender in 4 to 6 minutes and breasts in 6 to 8 minutes. Time is about doubled under low pressure (5 to 7 psi). **Mixed parts should not be steamed together.** Watch times carefully because over-cooking can occur easily in pressure steaming. The higher heat of steaming yields a slightly tougher flesh than does poaching. A small quantity of water in the pan helps when steaming poultry.

Barbecued Chicken

Yield: 4 servings

INGREDIENTS NEEDED
2 broiling chickens, approx. 2 lb each
⅓ c cider vinegar
1 tsp Worcestershire sauce
½ tsp onion salt
¼ tsp garlic salt
½ tsp salt
⅛ tsp pepper
Dash paprika
1 tbsp tomato paste
½ c melted fat

EQUIPMENT NEEDED
Cutting board
French knife
Liquid and dry measures
Pastry brush
Small saucepan
Bowl
Wire whip

PROCEDURE

1. Halve chickens by splitting down back.
2. Clean chickens thoroughly.
3. Brush with melted fat and place on preheated broiling rack, skin side down.
4. Place rack about 5 inches from heat source.
5. Broil approximately 15 minutes. Turn chicken, brush with fat, and broil on other side.
6. Turn again so skin side is down.
7. Allow 45 minutes for broiling chickens.
8. To prepare sauce, combine remaining ingredients in bowl and mix thoroughly with wire whip.
9. During broiling process, baste chicken with sauce using pastry brush.
10. Serve immediately.

Chicken Breasts with Yogurt Sauce

Yield: 6 servings

INGREDIENTS NEEDED

6 chicken breasts, boned
½ c butter or margarine
Salt and pepper to taste
½ tsp paprika
6 fresh scallions, chopped
¼ c parsley, minced
2 c chicken stock
Juice of 1 lemon
1 lb mushrooms, sliced
2 c plain yogurt
1 c walnuts, coarsely ground

EQUIPMENT NEEDED

Cutting board
French knife
Boning knife
Large skillet with cover
Serving platter

PROCEDURE

1. Debone chicken breasts and clean thoroughly.
2. Melt butter in skillet. Add chicken and season with salt, pepper, and paprika. Brown on both sides.
3. Add scallions, parsley, chicken stock, and lemon juice; bring to a boil. Reduce heat and simmer covered about 20 minutes, or until chicken is tender.
4. Remove chicken and arrange on serving platter.
5. Add mushrooms to stock. Simmer uncovered 3 minutes. Blend in yogurt and walnuts. (If sauce is too thick, dilute with a little stock or water.) Heat yogurt until just warm; **do not boil.**
6. Pour sauce over chicken and serve immediately.

Smothered Stuffed Chicken

Yield: 4 to 6 servings

INGREDIENTS NEEDED

1 chicken, approx. 3 lb
½ tsp salt
⅛ tsp pepper
2 tbsp butter or margarine
1¼ c dry bread cubes or pieces
¼ c onion, chopped
½ tsp dill weed
¼ c hot milk
⅓ c butter or margarine, melted

EQUIPMENT NEEDED

Cutting board
French knife
Liquid and dry measures
Small sauté pan
Poultry pins or skewers
Shallow roasting pan
Pastry brush
Aluminum foil
Oven, preheated to 350°F

PROCEDURE

1. Wash and clean chicken thoroughly, concentrating on cavity.
2. Sprinkle inside of chicken with salt and pepper. Tuck wing tips underneath wings. Chop liver.
3. Sauté liver lightly in 2 tablespoons butter for 2 minutes. Add bread cubes, onion, dill, and milk; mix well.
4. Stuff chicken. Close and secure with poultry pins or skewers.
5. Place in roasting pan.
6. Pour melted butter or margarine over chicken, and cover with foil.
7. Bake at 350°F about 1 hour, or until chicken is tender.
8. Remove cover and baste with excess butter or margarine. Increase temperature to 450°F.
9. Bake 10 minutes longer to brown evenly.
10. Serve immediately.

Fried Chicken

Yield: 3 or 4 servings

INGREDIENTS NEEDED	EQUIPMENT NEEDED
1 frying chicken, approx. 3 lb	*Cutting board*
½ c all-purpose flour	*French knife*
1½ tsp salt	*Liquid and dry measures*
¼ tsp pepper	*Wire whip*
Vegetable oil	*Mixing bowl*
2 eggs, well beaten	*Large, heavy skillet with lid*
¼ c milk	*Tongs*
1 tbsp parsley, chopped	*Paper towels*
½ c grated Parmesan cheese	*Plastic bag*
1 to 2 tbsp water	

PROCEDURE

1. Rinse and clean chicken thoroughly; pat dry with paper towels. To coat chicken evenly, shake 2 or 3 pieces at a time in a plastic bag containing flour, salt, and pepper.
2. Fill skillet ½ inch deep with vegetable oil; place over medium heat.
3. Combine eggs, milk, and parsley. Dip each chicken piece in egg mixture and roll in cheese. Starting with meaty pieces, place chicken skin side down in hot oil. Turn pieces as necessary to brown evenly on all sides.
4. When chicken is browned, reduce heat, pour in water, and cover pan tightly.
5. Cook chicken slowly 25 to 40 minutes, or until all pieces are tender. For crisp skin, uncover chicken during last 10 minutes of cooking.

Roast Rock Cornish Hen with Wild Rice and Mushrooms

Yield: 4 to 8 servings

INGREDIENTS NEEDED

1½ c water
½ tsp salt
½ c wild rice
2 tbsp butter or margarine
½ lb mushrooms, sliced lengthwise through caps and stems
1 tbsp onion, chopped fine
3 tbsp melted butter or margarine
2 tbsp Madeira wine
4 Rock Cornish game hens, 1 each
2 tsp salt
¼ c unsalted butter, melted
Watercress (optional)

EQUIPMENT NEEDED

Cutting board
French knife
Liquid and dry measures
Deep, heavy saucepan
Sieve or fine colander
Skillet
Absorbent paper
Skewers
Roasting pan with rack
Pastry brush
Sewing cord
Oven, preheated to 350°F

PROCEDURE

1. Bring water and salt to a boil in saucepan.
2. Wash rice in sieve. Add rice gradually to water so that boiling will not stop. Boil rapidly, covered, 30 to 40 minutes, or until a kernel of rice is entirely tender when pressed between fingers. Drain rice in colander or sieve.
3. While rice is cooking, heat 2 tablespoons butter or margarine in skillet. Add mushrooms and onion; cook, stirring occasionally, until mushrooms are lightly browned. Combine mushrooms, rice, melted butter, and wine; toss gently until mushrooms and butter are evenly distributed throughout rice.
4. Rinse and pat hens with absorbent paper. Rub cavities of hens with salt. Lightly fill body cavities with wild rice stuffing. To close body cavities, sew or skewer and lace with cord. With skewers, fasten neck skin to backs, and wings to bodies.
5. Place hens breast side up on rack in roasting pan. Brush each hen with melted unsalted butter (about 1 tablespoon).
6. Roast, uncovered, in 350°F oven; baste hens frequently during roasting period with drippings from roasting pan. Roast 1 to 1½ hours or until hens test done.
7. To test, move leg gently by grasping the end bone; drumstick-thigh joint moves easily when hen is done. Remove skewers if used.

Glazed Duckling Gourmet

Yield: 6 to 8 servings

INGREDIENTS NEEDED

2 ducklings approx. 4 lb each, quartered
(do not use wings, necks, and backs)
and skinned
1½ tsp salt
¼ tsp ground nutmeg
3 to 4 tbsp butter
1 clove garlic, minced
1½ tsp rosemary, crushed
1½ tsp thyme
1½ c burgundy wine
2 tsp red wine vinegar
⅓ c currant jelly
2 tsp cornstarch
2 tbsp cold water
1½ c halved seedless green grapes
Watercress (optional)

EQUIPMENT NEEDED

Cutting board
French knife
Liquid and dry measures
Absorbent paper
Large skillet with lid
Serving platter
Wire whip

PROCEDURE

1. Remove excess fat from duckling pieces; rinse duckling and pat dry with absorbent paper.
    Rub pieces with salt and nutmeg.
2. Heat butter and garlic in skillet over medium heat; add duckling pieces, and brown well on
    all sides.
3. Add rosemary, thyme, burgundy, vinegar, and jelly to skillet. Bring to a boil; cover and sim-
    mer over low heat until duckling is tender (about 45 minutes). Remove duckling and place
    on a platter.
4. Combine cornstarch and water; blend into liquid in skillet; bring to a boil and cook 1 to 2
    minutes, stirring constantly. Add grapes and toss lightly until thoroughly heated.
5. Pour hot sauce over duckling; garnish platter with watercress.

PRODUCT EVALUATION SHEET

Name _____ Lab date _____

Product prepared_____ Total prep time _____

Cooking method_____

Describe the following in one or two short sentences.

APPEARANCE (size, shape, consistency, etc.):

COLOR (golden brown, pasty white, bright, dull, etc.):

TEXTURE (smooth, lumpy, fine, coarse, sticky, gummy, etc.):

FLAVOR (sweet, sour, bitter, strong, spicy, bland, etc.):

TEMPERATURE (warm, hot, cold . . . Is it appropriate for the product?):

PROBLEMS ENCOUNTERED:

SOLUTION:
Suggestions to alter or improve the product:
1.

2.

Rating (10 being perfect):

0   1   2   3   4   5   6   7   8   9   10

17

Meat

Meat is any edible portion of cattle, swine, or sheep. It is a nutritious food that should be part of most diets. Further, the entrée of a menu is usually the meat; it dictates what other foods will be served as accompaniment. Beef, because of its lower fat content, is the most popular meat in this country. Pork, veal, and lamb (or mutton) follow in order.

Meat requires proper preparation. Improper handling or cooking can easily ruin it. Certain cuts need special cooking to be palatable and look attractive.

Kinds of Meat

Beef

Beef animals include veal and calves, steers, heifers, cows, stags, bulls, and bullocks. They are described as follows:

Veal. A young animal, 4 to 13 weeks old. Veal often comes from young dairy males. A veal carcass weighs from 75 to 300 pounds and yields about 40 percent edible meat, compared with 48 percent for beef. The flesh of veal is a delicate brownish pink and has very little fat.

Calf. Older than veal; 14 to 52 weeks old. Calf meat is beginning to turn to the typical rich beef red, but it is paler and has less fat. Calf is sometimes called **baby beef,** but the latter term should be applied only to older calves and to animals that have just moved out of the age range for calves.

Steer. A castrated male.

Heifer. A female that has never borne a calf. Heifers and steers are from 17 to 24 months old and are marketed as carcasses (around 1,000 pounds). Steers have more meat, but heifers have smaller bones, so the edible portion (EP yield) is about the same.

Cow. A female that has borne a calf.

Stag. A male castrated after maturity.

Bull. A mature male, not castrated.

Bullock. A young bull. Beef from bullocks came on the market about 1975. It was allowed to be called "bullock" and be graded Prime if the quality was indeed prime.

Male beef cattle are allowed to mature and become young bulls before being slaughtered for meat because they develop more flesh than do steers. They must be differentiated on the market, and their flesh has a slightly different flavor than that of steers or heifers. Foodservice operations use cows, stags, and bulls primarily for ground beef and other processed meats.

Pork

Much pork is cured. Pork animals include barrows, gilts, boars, and sows, described as follows:

Barrow. A young castrated male.

Gilt. A young unbred female.

These animals are around 6 months old when slaughtered, although good pork also comes from animals up to a year old. The typical weight is 220 pounds, of which 55 percent is edible meat.

Boar. A mature male.

Sow. A mature female.

These animals are quite fat and are usually used for sausage meat.

Lamb and Mutton

Lamb and mutton animals include lambs, ewes, rams, wethers, and yearlings. They are described as follows:

Lamb. A sheep from 6 months to 1 year old. Carcass weight is around 100 pounds, of which 35 percent is edible meat.

Mutton. Meat from a sheep more than 1 year old. Mutton flesh is fatter and darker and has a stronger flavor.

Ewe. A mature female.

Ram. A mature male.

Wether. A castrated young male.

Yearling. A 1-year-old (between lamb and mutton in quality).

The older animals are used for processed meats. Mutton is more popular as a table meat in England than in this country.

Inspection and Grading

Inspection establishes the fitness of meat for human consumption; **grading** concerns its palatability and yield.

Meat inspection is required by law in every plant in the United States. Animals—and the meat processed from them in any slaughterhouse or processing plant—must be produced in clean surroundings and must meet rigid standards for wholesomeness and sanitation. Inspection is carried out under municipal, state, or federal auspices. Local standards must meet or exceed federal ones.

Grading of beef is not mandatory. A packer can decide whether to have carcasses federally graded. No grading service is available for pork, although most packers follow the pork grades set by the government.

There are two kinds of grading: for quality (palatability) and for yield (percent of edible meat cuts). Veal carcasses are graded only as to quality. Lamb and mutton may be graded for either quality or yield. Pork, if the government grades are used, is graded as to quality, and these grades indicate the yield.

The following sections describe the meat grades assigned by the United States Department of Agriculture (USDA). The chart on page 109 shows the USDA grades for various kinds of meat.

Beef Grades

Following are the USDA grades for beef (including veal and calf):

Prime. The highest grade, produced in limited quantities. Its principal market is the so-called tablecloth restaurant trade, as well as meat shops and gourmet stores. Prime is most suitable for the natural "aging" process because it has a thick fat cover. (In aging, natural enzymes promote tenderizing and flavor development.)

Choice. The most popular grade in butcher shops and supermarkets. It is also widely distributed in the restaurant trade. As long as it has been economically feasible to produce it, because of abundant and inexpensive grain supplies, the customer demand for Choice quality has been filled. Choice is leaner than Prime but still can be aged moderately.

Good, Standard. Below Choice on the grading scale. Normally these grades contain less fat and are more apt to carry the store brand as "economy meat" where available. Good generally is not as flavorful, juicy, or tender as Choice; likewise, Standard falls below Good in palatability

USDA GRADES FOR MEAT

BEEF	VEAL (CALF)	LAMB	MUTTON	PORK
Prime	Prime	Prime	Choice	U.S. No. 1
Choice	Choice	Choice	Good	U.S. No. 2
Good	Good	Good	Utility	U.S. No. 3
Standard	Standard	Utility	Cull	U.S. No. 4
Commercial	Utility	Cull	***	Utility
Utility	Cull	***	***	***
Cutter	***	***	***	***
Canner	***	***	***	***

characteristics. Still, both have pleasing flavor, though milder than Choice and Prime grades.

Commercial, Cutter, Canner, Utility, Cull. Usually purchased by processors for conversion into ground beef or processing into sausage, cold cuts, canned stew, luncheon loaf, or other manufactured meat items. Though nutritious and wholesome, these grades lack the palatability characteristics of higher grades. However, this is not a problem because the cuts almost always are ground or precooked. The more tender of these cuts (ribs and loins) are featured in many popular low-cost "steakhouses."

Pork Grades

USDA grades for pork reflect only two levels of quality: acceptable and unacceptable. Unacceptable quality pork—which includes meat that is soft and watery—is graded U.S. Utility. All higher grades must have lean meat of acceptable quality.

The differences between these higher grades, which are numerical and range from U.S. No. 1 to U.S. No. 4, are solely a reflection of the yield of the four major lean cuts. In this respect they are similar to the yield grades for beef and lamb.

Cuts of Meat

Cuts of meat vary in quality and in the way they are purchased. The meat buyer must know the different cuts of meat. When buying meat, you should specify the name of the cut, the weight or portion size desired, and the maximum fat thickness, plus the grade or brand name.

Beef

A beef carcass is divided down the back to yield two sides. A side is split between the 12th and 13th ribs (Chicago cut) to yield a hindquarter and forequarter, which weigh about the same.

Following are cuts from the forequarter:

Chuck. Contains the first five ribs. From the shoulder part of the forequarter, it is 26 percent of the total carcass and yields about 75 to 85 percent usable meat.

If the foreshank and brisket are attached, it is a **cross-cut chuck.** With only the foreshank, it is an **armbone chuck.** With the foreshank and brisket cut away, it is a **square-cut chuck.**

The chuck is used for pot roasts, moist-cooked steaks, stewing meat, and ground beef. On the menu, chuck dishes include pot roast, salisbury steak, beef stew, beef ragout, and meat loaf. The chuck contains the **clod,** which sits over the blade bone.

Rib. Contains seven rib bones, 6 through 12, and is considered the best forequarter cut. The average rib weighs from 20 to 25 pounds and is 75 to 85 percent usable meat.

Roast ribs of beef, rib (Delmonico) steaks, the eye of the rib roast, and short ribs come from the rib.

Shank. Usually ground for ground beef or used for stews.

Brisket. Used for corned beef and pastrami.

Short plate. At the top, yields short ribs; at the bottom, yields boiling beef or ground meat.

Following are cuts from the hindquarter:

Round. Accounts for 23 percent of the carcass. The round can be subdivided into the rump, top (inside) round, bottom (outside) round, knuckle or sirloin tip, and hind shank.

The inside round cut is the most tender cut from the round, and from quite young animals it will be very tender. The knuckle also can be used for a dry heat roast if it comes from good-quality beef.

The rest of the round should be cooked by moist heat cooking methods. Swiss steaks, stews, pot roasts, beef roulades, and cube steaks are made from the round.

A steamship round, which is the whole round with the rump and shank cut off, often is roasted whole for buffets. It should come from a very good quality animal and weigh about 50 pounds, which can serve nearly 80 persons heartily.

Sirloin or loin end. Accounts for about 9 percent of the carcass. Sirloin steaks can be dry-heat cooked. The bottom butt and top butt sirloin steaks are popular foodservice items. Even though slightly chewy, they have excellent flavor. The sirloin can also be dry-heat roasted. The butt tenderloin makes a fairly large tenderloin steak.

Short loin. Contains the strip or loin eye and the tenderloin. The cut can be boned out to make New York strip steaks and a boneless tenderloin. The strip and tenderloin sometimes are dry-heat roasted. If unboned, the steaks at the 13th rib (next to the rib on the forequarter) make the club or Delmonico steaks; next come the T-bone steak and the porterhouse.

Flank. A muscle that lies imbedded in fat below the loin and loin end. It is about 5 percent of the total carcass. The flank is stripped from its fatty tissue and used for London broil, a steak that is broiled rare and served thinly sliced au jus. Swiss

steaks, stews, and ground beef also can be made from flank.

Figure 17-1 shows retail cuts of beef.

Pork

A side of pork is half of the carcass. Foodservice operations usually purchase the loin rather than the side. Following are pork cuts:

Leg. Also called the ham; contains the rump and part of the sirloin. The leg can be boned and used for a roast or can be roasted bone in with dry heat.

Pork steaks also come from the ham. The leg often is cured and smoked to make cured, smoked ham, which also can be baked or cut into ham steaks.

Shank. From either a fresh or a cured and smoked leg. It can be cooked with meats or vegetables.

Loin. The rib and loin, including the sirloin; used for roasts and for pork chops. The blade chops come from the area of the shoulder blade; the center cut chops, and then the loin chops, come from the other end. The tenderloin can be removed from the loin and used for very tender cutlets.

Boston butt or shoulder. The upper part of the shoulder, containing the blade bone. The butt can be sliced into steaks or boned and made into a boneless roast.

Picnic. The lower half of the shoulder. Picnics are rather bony and usually are boiled.

Both the butt and picnic can be cured and smoked.

Jowl. The face meat of the hog. It can be purchased fresh and used for frying, as fresh bacon is used. The jowl also can be cured and smoked and used as bacon is.

See Figure 17-2 for the retail cuts of pork.

Veal

Veal is cut in half between the 12th and 13th ribs. Unlike beef, it usually is not divided into

RETAIL CUTS OF BEEF
WHERE THEY COME FROM AND HOW TO COOK THEM

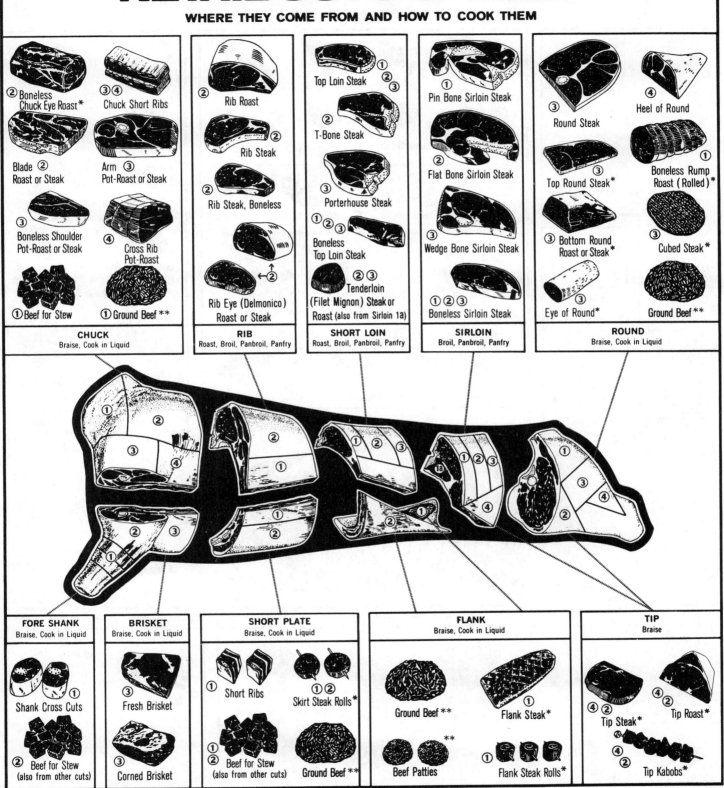

CHUCK
Braise, Cook in Liquid

RIB
Roast, Broil, Panbroil, Panfry

SHORT LOIN
Roast, Broil, Panbroil, Panfry

SIRLOIN
Broil, Panbroil, Panfry

ROUND
Braise, Cook in Liquid

CHUCK
- ② Boneless Chuck Eye Roast *
- ③④ Chuck Short Ribs
- Blade ② Roast or Steak
- Arm ③ Pot-Roast or Steak
- ③ Boneless Shoulder Pot-Roast or Steak
- ④ Cross Rib Pot-Roast
- ① Beef for Stew
- ① Ground Beef **

RIB
- ② Rib Roast
- ② Rib Steak
- ② Rib Steak, Boneless
- Rib Eye (Delmonico) Roast or Steak

SHORT LOIN
- ①② ③ Top Loin Steak
- ② T-Bone Steak
- ③ Porterhouse Steak
- ①②③ Boneless Top Loin Steak
- ②③ Tenderloin (Filet Mignon) Steak or Roast (also from Sirloin 1a)

SIRLOIN
- ① Pin Bone Sirloin Steak
- ② Flat Bone Sirloin Steak
- ③ Wedge Bone Sirloin Steak
- ①②③ Boneless Sirloin Steak

ROUND
- ③ Round Steak
- ④ Heel of Round
- ③ Top Round Steak *
- ① Boneless Rump Roast (Rolled) *
- ③ Bottom Round Roast or Steak *
- ③ Cubed Steak *
- ③ Eye of Round *
- ③ Ground Beef **

FORE SHANK
Braise, Cook in Liquid
- ① Shank Cross Cuts
- ② Beef for Stew (also from other cuts)

BRISKET
Braise, Cook in Liquid
- ③ Fresh Brisket
- ③ Corned Brisket

SHORT PLATE
Braise, Cook in Liquid
- ① Short Ribs
- ①② Skirt Steak Rolls *
- ①② Beef for Stew (also from other cuts)
- ①② Ground Beef **

FLANK
Braise, Cook in Liquid
- Ground Beef **
- ① Flank Steak *
- ** Beef Patties
- ① Flank Steak Rolls *

TIP
Braise
- ④② Tip Steak *
- ④② Tip Roast *
- ④② Tip Kabobs *

*May be Roasted, Broiled, Panbroiled or Panfried from high quality beef.
**May be Roasted, (Baked), Broiled, Panbroiled or Panfried.

This chart approved by
National Live Stock and Meat Board

© National Live Stock and Meat Board

FIGURE 17-1   Beef Chart (Photo courtesy of the National Livestock and Meat Board.)

RETAIL CUTS OF PORK

WHERE THEY COME FROM AND HOW TO COOK THEM

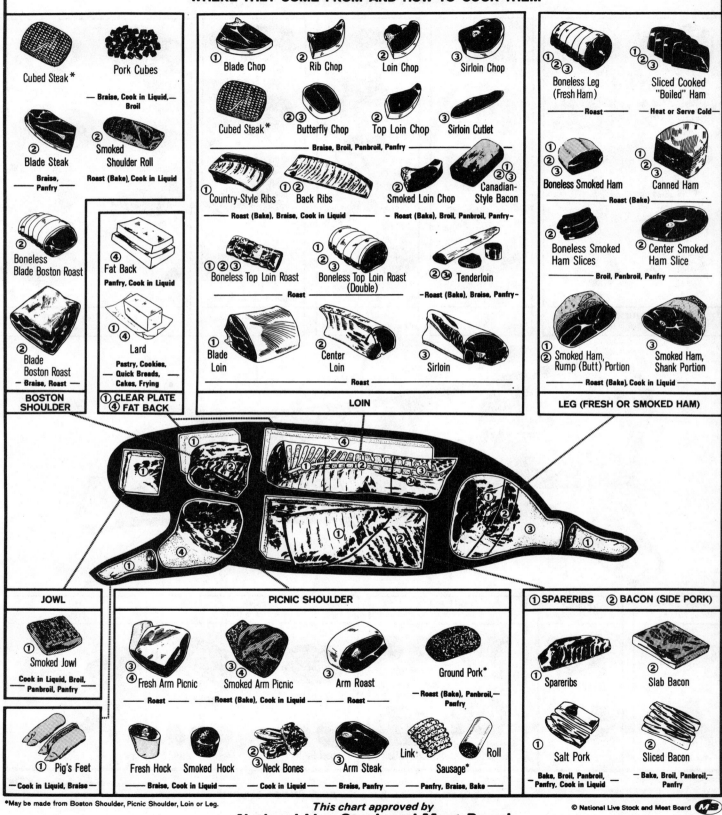

This chart approved by
National Live Stock and Meat Board

© National Live Stock and Meat Board

*May be made from Boston Shoulder, Picnic Shoulder, Loin or Leg.

FIGURE 17-2   Pork Chart (Photo courtesy of the National Livestock and Meat Board.)

sides or quarters. The front part is called the foresaddle, and the back part is called the hindsaddle.

Following are cuts from the foresaddle:

Shoulder. Includes 5 rib bones. It is used for stews, veal steaks, and roasting.

Hotel rack or rib. Includes 7 ribs. The crown roast or rib roast can be made from the rib cut. Rib steaks also can be taken from it.

Breast. The shank, brisket, and foreplate. These cuts can be used for stews, converted to ground veal, boned and rolled for roasts, or made into braising veal.

Following are cuts from the hindsaddle:

Leg. Accounts for 34 percent of the total carcass weight; includes the rump and the sirloin, as on beef. The leg can be used for steaks, chops, roasts, cutlets, stews, or ground veal.

Loin. Contains the loin eye and tenderloin. It is used for loin chops or roasts.

Flank. Can be used for stew or for ground veal. Figure 17-3 illustrates the retail cuts of veal.

Lamb

Lamb, like veal, is divided into the foresaddle, which is the front half of the carcass, and the hindsaddle, which in turn is divided into the leg and the loin.

Following are cuts from the foresaddle:

Shoulder. Contains the first five ribs and accounts for 26 percent of the carcass. The fairly high percentage of lean meat found here is cut for steaks, cubed for kabobs and stews, ground for patties, and sliced for curries. The popular hotel rack, or rib area of the carcass, often is prepared as a crown roast of lamb. The hotel rack also is cut into individual chops, each containing one rib and the lean meat of the rib eye.

Breast. Contains tips of 12 ribs and can be used for stew or ground meat. If boned, the breast can be rolled or stuffed as a roast.

Foreshank. Contains little lean meat but can be braised whole and served with vegetables as a veal shank might be served.

Following are cuts from the hindsaddle:

Leg. Contains solid, lean, fine-textured meat; usually weighs from 6 to 9 pounds. Roasts, steaks, and cubed or ground meat are all cut from the leg of lamb.

The American leg has the sirloin roast and shank bone removed, whereas the combination leg has just the shank bone removed.

Loin. The trimmed loin, or loin with the flank removed. A fairly popular cut, it accounts for approximately 7 percent of the carcass weight. Lamb chops usually are cut from the loin. Some operations also serve loin roasts. If the loin is untrimmed and taken from the whole lamb carcass unsplit, English lamb chops can be cut. These chops are 2 inches thick and are twice the size of normal lamb chops.

Much of the lamb today is purchased in fabricated cuts or in ready-to-cook form. These cuts are uniform in weight, easy to store, and labor-saving, but they are usually more expensive. The cost consideration must be weighed against the meat-cutting skill of your personnel, the cutting equipment and storage space available, and the products to be served. Figure 17-4 shows the retail cuts of lamb.

Variety Meats

Variety meats can be made into excellent dishes that yield a good gross profit margin. Following are the most common variety meats:

Liver. The most widely used variety or organ meat. Calves' liver is the most tender and delicate. Beef liver is heavier in flavor and can be somewhat tough; it frequently is braised. Pork and lamb liver are also available.

Sweetbreads. Small glands taken from veal and calves. A true sweetbread comes from only the thymus gland in the neck, but other glands are also used. Sweetbreads can be served in many popular dishes.

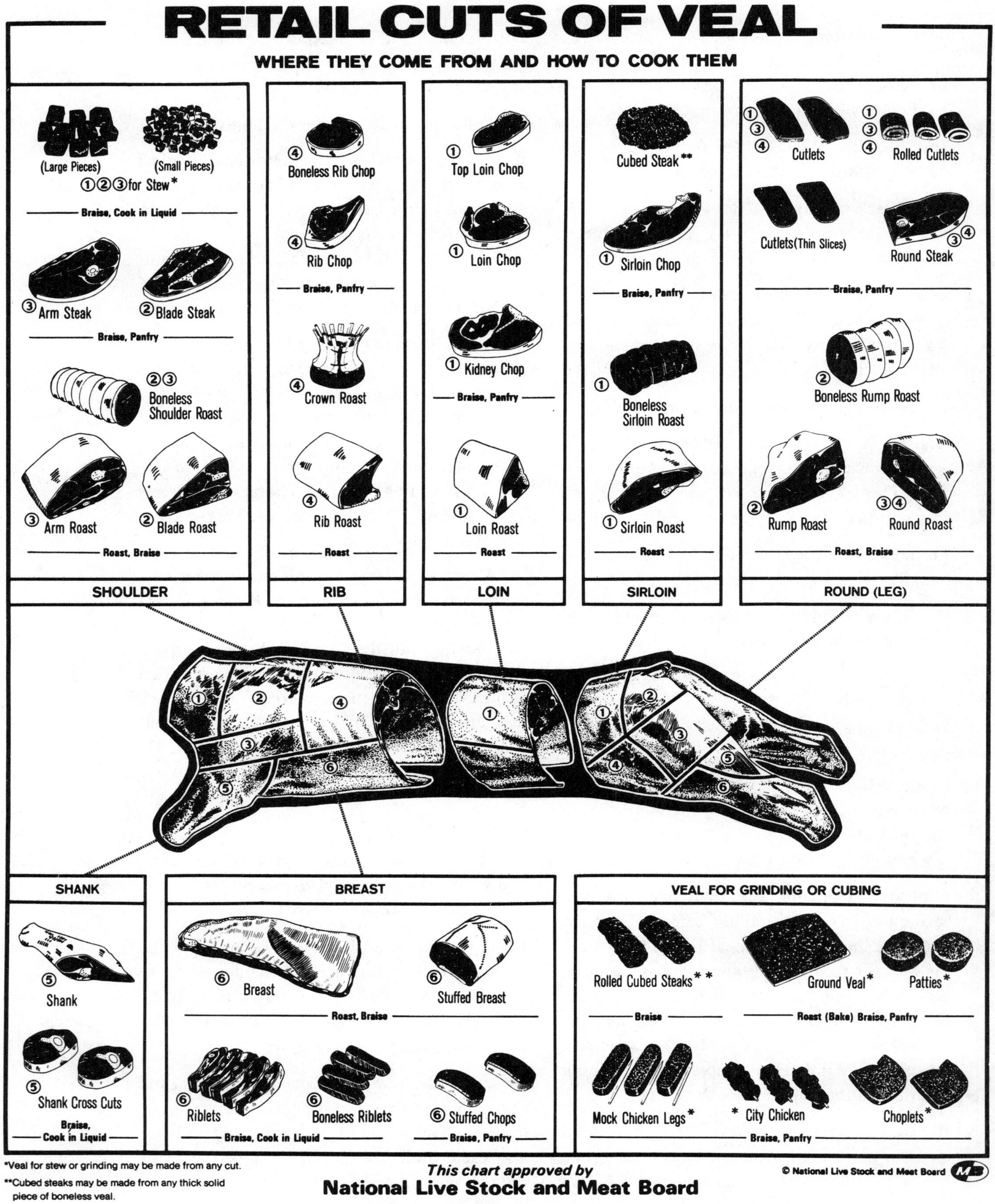

RETAIL CUTS OF VEAL
WHERE THEY COME FROM AND HOW TO COOK THEM

SHOULDER

(Large Pieces)   (Small Pieces)
① ② ③ for Stew *
— Braise, Cook in Liquid —
③ Arm Steak   ② Blade Steak
— Braise, Panfry —
② ③ Boneless Shoulder Roast
③ Arm Roast   ② Blade Roast
— Roast, Braise —

RIB

④ Boneless Rib Chop
④ Rib Chop
— Braise, Panfry —
④ Crown Roast
④ Rib Roast
— Roast —

LOIN

① Top Loin Chop
① Loin Chop
① Kidney Chop
— Braise, Panfry —
① Loin Roast
— Roast —

SIRLOIN

Cubed Steak **
① Sirloin Chop
— Braise, Panfry —
① Boneless Sirloin Roast
① Sirloin Roast
— Roast —

ROUND (LEG)

① ③ ④ Cutlets   ① ③ ④ Rolled Cutlets
Cutlets (Thin Slices)   ③ ④ Round Steak
— Braise, Panfry —
② Boneless Rump Roast
② Rump Roast   ③ ④ Round Roast
— Roast, Braise —

SHANK

⑤ Shank
⑤ Shank Cross Cuts
— Braise, Cook in Liquid —

BREAST

⑥ Breast
⑥ Stuffed Breast
— Roast, Braise —
⑥ Riblets   ⑥ Boneless Riblets   ⑥ Stuffed Chops
— Braise, Cook in Liquid —   — Braise, Panfry —

VEAL FOR GRINDING OR CUBING

Rolled Cubed Steaks **   Ground Veal *   Patties *
— Braise —   — Roast (Bake) Braise, Panfry —
Mock Chicken Legs *   * City Chicken   Choplets *
— Braise, Panfry —

*Veal for stew or grinding may be made from any cut.

**Cubed steaks may be made from any thick solid piece of boneless veal.

This chart approved by
National Live Stock and Meat Board

© National Live Stock and Meat Board

FIGURE 17-3   Veal Chart (Photo courtesy of the National Livestock and Meat Board.)

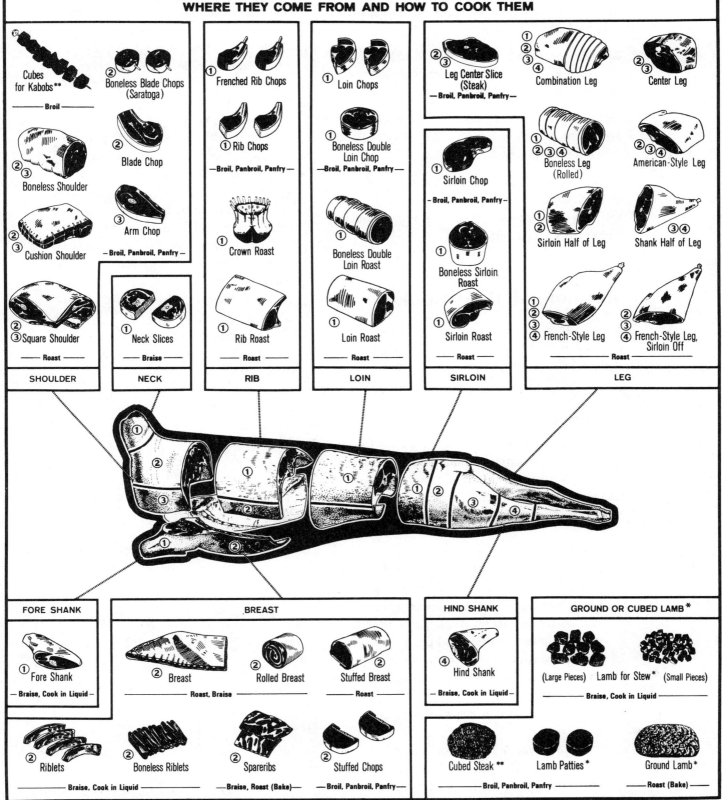

RETAIL CUTS OF LAMB
WHERE THEY COME FROM AND HOW TO COOK THEM

SHOULDER

Cubes for Kabobs**
— Broil —

Boneless Blade Chops (Saratoga)

Blade Chop

Arm Chop

Boneless Shoulder

Cushion Shoulder

— Broil, Panbroil, Panfry —

Square Shoulder

— Roast —

NECK

Neck Slices

— Braise —

RIB

Frenched Rib Chops

Rib Chops

— Broil, Panbroil, Panfry —

Crown Roast

Rib Roast

— Roast —

LOIN

Loin Chops

Boneless Double Loin Chop

— Broil, Panbroil, Panfry —

Boneless Double Loin Roast

Loin Roast

— Roast —

SIRLOIN

Sirloin Chop

— Broil, Panbroil, Panfry —

Boneless Sirloin Roast

Sirloin Roast

— Roast —

Leg Center Slice (Steak)
— Broil, Panbroil, Panfry —

Combination Leg

Center Leg

Boneless Leg (Rolled)

American-Style Leg

Sirloin Half of Leg

Shank Half of Leg

French-Style Leg

French-Style Leg, Sirloin Off

LEG
— Roast —

FORE SHANK

Fore Shank

— Braise, Cook in Liquid —

Riblets

— Braise, Cook in Liquid —

BREAST

Breast

Rolled Breast

Stuffed Breast

— Roast, Braise — — Roast —

Boneless Riblets

Spareribs

Stuffed Chops

— Braise, Cook in Liquid — — Braise, Roast (Bake) — — Broil, Panbroil, Panfry —

HIND SHANK

Hind Shank

— Braise, Cook in Liquid —

GROUND OR CUBED LAMB*

(Large Pieces)   Lamb for Stew*   (Small Pieces)

— Braise, Cook in Liquid —

Cubed Steak**

Lamb Patties*

Ground Lamb*

— Broil, Panbroil, Panfry — — Roast (Bake) —

* Lamb for stew or grinding may be made from any cut.

**Kabobs or cubed steaks may be made from any thick solid piece of boneless Lamb.

This chart approved by
National Live Stock and Meat Board

© National Live Stock and Meat Board

FIGURE 17-4   Lamb Chart (Photo courtesy of the National Livestock and Meat Board.)

Brains. Can be cooked and then diced and recooked with scrambled eggs, or dredged in flour and sautéed in butter.

Kidneys. Often left in lamb, veal, calf, and mutton. Beef kidney usually is simmered and then used for steak and kidney pie.

Tongue. From all meat animals. Tongue can be used fresh, cured, or cured and smoked. Moist cooking is necessary.

Tripe. The muscular lining of the first stomach of beef. Used for soups, it also can be braised and served in sauce. Tripe is a very popular "nationality" type entrée.

Methods of Meat Cookery

A wide variety of methods may be used in meat cookery. Refer to the glossary at the end of the chapter for a list of meat cooking terms.

Roasting

Roasting is a dry heat method used to cook foods by surrounding them with hot, dry air, usually in an oven. No water is used, and the meat is left uncovered so that steam can escape. Following are the basic procedures for roasting meats:

1. Assemble all equipment and food supplies. Select a roasting pan that has low sides (so moisture vapor does not collect around the roast) and that is just large enough to hold the roast. If the pan is too large, drippings will spread out too thin and burn.
2. Prepare or trim meat for roasting. Heavy fat coverings should be trimmed to about ½ inch thick.
3. If desired, season the meat several hours ahead or the day before.
4. Place the meat fat side up on a rack in the roasting pan. The rack holds the roast out of the drippings. Bones may be used if no rack is available. A bone-in rib roast needs no rack because the bones act as a natural rack.

5. Insert a clean and sanitary meat thermometer so that the bulb is in the center mass of the meat, not touching bone or fat.
6. Do not cover or add water to the pan. Roasting is a dry heat cooking method.
7. Place meat in a preheated oven.
8. Roast to desired doneness, allowing for carryover cooking.
9. If desired, add mirepoix to the pan during the last half of the cooking period.
10. Remove the roast from the oven and let stand in a warm place 15 to 30 minutes.
11. If the meat must be held, place it in an oven or warmer set no higher than the desired internal temperature of the roast.
12. While the roast is resting, prepare jus or pan gravy from drippings. Mirepoix may be added to the drippings now if it was not added in step 9.
13. Slice the roast as close as possible to serving time. Generally, slice the meat against the grain for tenderness.

Products that lend themselves to roasting are large, tender cuts such as . . .

▼ Meat loaf
▼ Beef roasts
▼ Pork, lamb, veal
▼ Poultry
▼ Fish

The following chart shows the proper roasting temperatures for various kinds of meat.

ROASTING TEMPERATURES	
300°F–325°F	Beef, veal, lamb, cured pork
350°	Fresh pork

Broiling

Broiling is a dry heat method that uses very high heat to cook meat quickly. Properly broiled meat has a well-browned, flavorful crust on the outside. The inside is cooked to the desired doneness and is still juicy. It may be helpful to think of broiling as a browning rather than a cooking technique because the best, juiciest broiled meats are those cooked to the rare or medium-done stage.

Because of the intense heat, it is difficult to broil meats to the well-done stage and still keep them juicy. Pork and veal, which are usually eaten well done, are generally better griddled, sautéed, or braised than broiled. (Veal can be broiled successfully if the customer prefers it still pink inside.)

Here are the basic procedures for broiling:

1. Assemble and prepare all equipment and food supplies. If necessary, score the fatty edges of meat to prevent curling.
2. Preheat the broiler.
3. Dip the meat in oil, let excess drip off, and place the meat on the broiler. The oil helps prevent sticking and keeps the product moist. (This step may be unnecessary for meats that are high in fat.) **Using too much oil can cause grease fires.**
4. When one side is brown and the meat is cooked halfway, turn it over with tongs. Never use a fork or utensil that will pierce the meat and cause it to lose its juices.
5. Cook the second side until the meat is cooked to the desired doneness.
6. Remove from broiler and serve immediately.

Products that lend themselves to broiling are small, tender cuts of meats such as . . .

▼ Steaks
▼ Ham and bacon
▼ Lamb chops
▼ Ground meat patties

Sautéing, Panfrying, and Griddling

Sautéing, panfrying, and griddling are range top methods using varying amounts of fat. Following are general guidelines for all of these methods:

1. Use only tender cuts for sautéing.
2. Smaller or thinner pieces of meat require higher heat. The object is to brown or sear the meat in the time it takes to cook it to the desired doneness. Very small or thin pieces cook in just a few moments.
3. If large or thick items are browned over high heat, it may be necessary to finish them at lower heat to avoid burning them.
4. The amount of fat needed is the amount required to conduct the heat to all surfaces so that the item cooks evenly. Flat items need much less fat than irregularly shaped items like chicken pieces.

PROCEDURES FOR SAUTÉING AND PANFRYING OR GRIDDLING

SAUTÉING

1. Assemble all equipment and food supplies.
2. Prepare meats as required. This may include dredging with flour.
3. Heat a small amount of fat in a sauté pan until very hot.
4. Add the meat to the pan. Do not overcrowd the pan.
5. Brown the meat on all sides, flipping or tossing it in the pan as necessary, so that it cooks evenly.
6. Remove meat from pan and drain excess fat.
7. Serve immediately.

PANFRYING OR GRIDDLING

1. Assemble all equipment and food supplies.
2. Prepare meats as required. This may include breading or dredging with flour.
3. Heat a moderate amount of fat in a sauté pan or skillet until hot.
4. Add the meat to the pan.
5. Brown the meat on one side. Turn it with a spatula and brown the other side. Larger pieces may need to be finished at reduced heat after browning. Or, if required, they may finish cooking uncovered, in the oven.
6. Serve immediately.

5. Sautéing small pieces of meat requires little fat because the items are tossed or flipped so that all sides come in contact with the hot pan.
6. When sautéing small pieces of food, do not overload the pan, and do not flip or toss the food more than necessary. Doing so will cause the temperature to drop too much, and the meat will simmer in its own juices instead of sautéing.
7. Use clarified butter or oil or a mixture for sautéing. Whole butter burns too easily.
8. Dredging meats in flour promotes even browning and helps prevent sticking. Flour meats immediately before cooking, not in advance, or the flour will get pasty. Shake off excess flour before adding meat to the pan.
9. When panfrying several batches, strain or skim the fat between batches. Otherwise, burned food particles from previous batches may mar the appearance of the meat.
10. For pork and veal chops, griddling and panfrying are preferable to broiling and grilling because the lower temperatures keep these meats moister when they are cooked well done. Hamburgers cooked well done are also moister if cooked on a griddle or grill.

The chart on page 117 gives the specific procedures for sautéing and panfrying and shows how they differ.

Pan Broiling

Cooking very thin steaks (such as minute steaks) to the rare stage is difficult because the heat is not high enough to form a good brown crust without overcooking the inside. Pan broiling in a heavy skillet is a solution to this problem. Follow these basic procedures:

1. Preheat an iron skillet over a high flame until it is very hot. (The pan should be well seasoned.) Do not add fat.
2. Proceed as in panfrying, but pour off any fat that accumulates during the cooking process if necessary.

Braising and Cooking in Liquid

A popular and delicious method of preparation is braising. Here are the procedures:

1. Assemble all equipment and food supplies.
2. Prepare the meat for cooking, as required.
3. Brown the meat thoroughly in a heavy pan with fat or in a hot oven.

MEAT COOKING TERMS

Braising: A cooking method that combines sautéing and simmering

Breaded: Covered with a coating of flour, egg wash, and bread crumbs

Broiling: A cooking method in which the food is exposed to direct heat

Deep-fat fry: To cook food by immersing it in hot fat

Deglaze: To remove crusted particles from a pan by adding liquid and swishing it around

Dredge: To coat with a dry ingredient such as flour

Grill: To cook on a flat surface on top of a heat source

Mirepoix: Roughly cut onions, celery, and carrots

Reduce: To let a liquid cook down until it is concentrated

Roast: To cook uncovered in an oven

Roux: A thickening agent made by cooking together equal parts of flour and fat

Sauté: To cook lightly in a small amount of butter or oil

Simmer: To cook just below the boiling point

Stewing: A moist heat method in which the cooking liquid becomes the sauce or gravy for the finished dish

BASIC METHODS OF MEAT COOKERY

COOKING BY DRY HEAT

Roasting

Broiling

Pan broiling

Griddling

COOKING BY MOIST HEAT

Braising

Cooking in liquid

COOKING WITH FAT

Panfrying

Deep-fat frying

Use low temperatures for all meats and all methods.

4. Remove the meat from the pan (if required), and brown mirepoix in the remaining fat.

5. Add flour to make a roux. Brown the roux.

6. Add stock to make a thickened sauce. Add seasonings and flavorings.

7. Return the meat to the pan. Cover and simmer in the oven or on the range until the meat is tender.

8. Adjust the sauce as necessary (strain, season, reduce, dilute, etc.).

Veal Scaloppine alla Marsala

Yield: 10 servings

INGREDIENTS NEEDED

2½ lb veal scaloppine: 20 pieces, 2 oz each
1 oz salt
1 oz white pepper
3 oz flour
½ c vegetable oil
4 oz marsala wine
8 oz strong stock
2 oz butter, cut in pieces
2 tbsp parsley, chopped

EQUIPMENT NEEDED

Meat mallet for tenderization
Absorbent paper towels
Large sauté pan
Small hotel pan for dredging
Liquid and dry measures
Ounce portion scale
French knife
Cutting board

PROCEDURE

1. Lightly flatten each piece of veal with a meat mallet. **Do not pound hard, or you may tear the meat.**
2. Dry meat, season it with salt and pepper, and dredge in flour. Shake off excess. **Do not do this step until immediately before cooking.**
3. Heat oil in sauté pan until very hot. Add veal and sauté over high heat just until lightly browned on both sides. (If necessary sauté the meat in several batches.)
4. Remove meat from pan and drain the excess oil.
5. Add marsala to the pan and deglaze.
6. Add stock and reduce over high heat by about half.
7. Add pieces of butter and swirl pan until they are melted and blended with sauce.
8. Add veal to the pan and bring just to a simmer. Turn meat to coat it with sauce.
9. Serve immediately, two pieces per portion, sprinkled with chopped parsley.

Note: **Brown sauce may be used instead of stock. But stock makes a more delicate product without masking the flavor of the veal.**

Stuffed Pork Chops

Yield: 6 servings

INGREDIENTS NEEDED
6 double pork chops
1½ c whole kernel corn
1½ c bread crumbs
¾ tsp salt
¼ tsp pepper
1½ tbsp parsley, minced
¾ tsp sage
1 tbsp grated onion
1 c diced apples
1 egg
3 tbsp milk
¼ c vegetable oil
Salt and pepper to taste

EQUIPMENT NEEDED
Boning knife
Liquid and dry measures
Cutting board
Heavy skillet
Small roasting pan
Oven, preheated to 350°F

PROCEDURE

1. Cut a pocket on bone side of each chop, using boning knife.
2. Combine remaining ingredients except oil and mix well.
3. Stuff each chop with corn mixture.
4. Brown chops in vegetable oil, season, and add a small amount of water.
5. Bake uncovered at 350°F for approximately 1 hour or until chops are tender.

Salisbury Steak

Yield: 6 servings

INGREDIENTS NEEDED
4 strips bacon, diced
1 tbsp onion, chopped
1 tbsp green pepper, chopped
1 tbsp parsley, chopped
1 tsp salt
½ tsp pepper
1½ lb ground beef (chuck or round)
½ lb ground pork

EQUIPMENT NEEDED
Cutting board
French knife
Dry measures
Tongs or metal spatula
Broiler
Portion scale

PROCEDURE

1. Mix bacon, onion, green pepper, parsley, salt, and pepper lightly with ground beef and pork, not mixing too much.
2. Shape mixture into oval steaks, weighing each for equal portion amounts.
3. Place steaks under broiler approximately 3 inches from heat source.
4. Broil for 12 minutes, turning the steaks only once, using tongs or a metal spatula.
5. Serve immediately.

Stir-Fry Beef and Broccoli

Yield: 6 servings

INGREDIENTS NEEDED

2 lb fresh broccoli
2 lb beef round or chuck, boneless
¼ c olive oil
2 cloves garlic, minced
3 c hot chicken broth
4 tsp cornstarch
¼ c cold water
3 tbsp soy sauce
1 tsp salt
2 cans (16 oz each) bean sprouts, drained and rinsed
4 c cooked white rice

EQUIPMENT NEEDED

Cutting board
Liquid and dry measures
French knife
Boning knife
Large, heavy sauté pan
Wire whip

PROCEDURE

1. Clean broccoli and cut into pieces about 2½ inches long and ¼ inch thick; set aside. Slice beef very thin and cut diagonally into 4 × ½-inch strips; set aside.
2. Heat 1 tablespoon oil with garlic in sauté pan. Add half of beef and stir-fry until evenly browned. Remove cooked meat from pan and stir-fry remaining beef, adding more oil if necessary.
3. Pour 1 tablespoon oil in pan. Add half of broccoli and stir-fry over high heat ½ minute. Remove cooked broccoli from pan and stir-fry remaining broccoli ½ minute, adding more oil if necessary.
4. Place all broccoli in sauté pan. Cover and cook 3 minutes. Remove broccoli and keep warm.
5. Blend into broth a mixture of cornstarch, cold water, soy sauce, and salt. Bring to a boil, stirring constantly, and cook until mixture thickens.
6. Add bean sprouts, broccoli, and beef; toss to mix. Heat thoroughly and serve over hot, fluffy rice.

Lamb Stew Continental

Yield: 6 servings

INGREDIENTS NEEDED

2 lb lamb shoulder, boneless, cut in 1½-in. cubes
2 tbsp vegetable oil
½ c onion, chopped
½ tsp salt
½ tsp basil
½ tsp oregano
1 bay leaf, crushed
1 can (16 oz) whole tomatoes, drained
1 can (8 oz) tomato sauce
2 cloves garlic
1 tsp sugar
½ green pepper, cut into strips

EQUIPMENT NEEDED

Cutting board
Liquid and dry measures
French knife
Boning knife
Large sauté pan with lid

PROCEDURE

1. Brown lamb cubes in vegetable oil in large sauté pan.
2. Add onion and cook, stirring frequently, until onion is soft.
3. Drain off excess fat. Add salt, basil, oregano, bay leaf, tomatoes, tomato sauce, garlic, and sugar. Simmer covered 1½ hours.
4. Add green pepper. Cover and simmer 15 minutes or until meat is tender.
5. Remove cover and cook, stirring as necessary, until sauce is reduced to desired consistency. Remove garlic.

Beef Burgundy

Yield: 7 servings

INGREDIENTS NEEDED	EQUIPMENT NEEDED
2 slices bacon	*French knife*
2 lb beef round tip steak, cut in 2-in. cubes	*Boning knife*
2 tbsp flour	*Cutting board*
1 tsp salt	*Liquid and dry measures*
1 tsp pepper	*Heavy stockpot with lid*
2 tsp garlic powder	*Fork*
2 tsp Italian seasoning	
1 c burgundy wine	
1 c water	
1 tbsp tomato paste	
12 small boiling onions	
4 oz mushrooms, sliced and lightly browned in 1 tbsp butter	
16 cherry tomatoes, stems removed	

PROCEDURE

1. Fry bacon in stockpot; remove bacon. Coat meat cubes with a blend of flour and salt. Add to fat in stockpot and brown thoroughly. Add pepper, garlic powder, Italian seasoning, burgundy, water, and tomato paste. Cover and simmer gently 45 minutes.

2. Peel onions and pierce each end with a fork so they will retain their shape when cooked. Add onions to beef mixture and simmer 40 minutes or until meat and onions are tender. Add mushrooms and cherry tomatoes; simmer 3 minutes.

3. Pour into a serving dish and serve immediately.

PRODUCT EVALUATION SHEET

Name _____   Lab date_____

Product prepared_____   Total prep time _____

Cooking method_____

Describe the following in one or two short sentences.

APPEARANCE (size, shape, consistency, etc.):

COLOR (golden brown, pasty white, bright, dull, etc.):

TEXTURE (smooth, lumpy, fine, coarse, sticky, gummy, etc.):

FLAVOR (sweet, sour, bitter, strong, spicy, bland, etc.):

TEMPERATURE (warm, hot, cold . . . Is it appropriate for the product?):

PROBLEMS ENCOUNTERED:

SOLUTION:
Suggestions to alter or improve the product:
1.

2.

Rating (10 being perfect):

0   1   2   3   4   5   6   7   8   9   10

18

Eggs

Structure of the Egg

You know that the egg is contained in a shell and consists of the white (**albumen**) and yellow portion (**yolk**). The shell of the egg is porous and permits moisture and gases to pass through. On the outside of the shell is a thin film called the **bloom,** which helps to seal the pores and protect the egg from contamination. The color of the shell will vary from white to brown, depending upon the breed of chicken that laid it. The color of the egg does not affect its cooking properties or palatability.

Between the shell and the egg white there are two membranes, **inner** and **outer,** which protect the quality of the egg. The white of the egg consists of the **thin** and **thick white.** Fresh eggs will contain more thick white than older eggs. The thick white gives the egg a high, rounded appearance when it is removed from the shell. Such an egg will make a more attractive fried or poached egg than one in which the white spreads out.

The **yolk membrane** separates the yolk from the white. Attached to the yolk membrane on each side is a rope or cord called the **chalaza,** which holds the yolk near the center of the egg. There is a light spot on the yolk known as the **germ spot,** which in a fertilized and incubated egg can develop into a baby chick. The yolk supplies the food for the growing embryo.

The color of the yolk depends upon the food the hen eats. In a fresh egg, the yolk is high and rounded and in the center of the thick white. An **air cell** appears at the blunt end of the egg; it gets bigger as the egg ages.

Figure 18-1 shows the structure of the egg.

Grade and Size

Most eggs sold are graded for freshness and size according to USDA standards. The process of grading for freshness is known as **candling,** which entails placing the egg in front of a very strong light beam in a darkened room. Twirling the egg in front of the light makes it possible to judge the thickness of the white, the size and position of the yolk, and the size of the air cell.

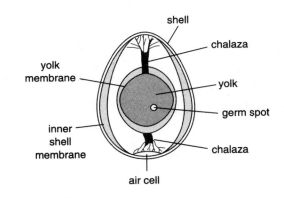

FIGURE 18-1   Egg Structure

EGG SIZES AND WEIGHTS	
CLASSIFICATION	WEIGHT PER DOZEN
Jumbo	30 oz
Extra large	27 oz
Large	24 oz
Medium	21 oz
Small	18 oz
Peewee	15 oz

The freshest egg has a thick white that supports the rounded, firm yolk and a small air cell.

Freshness of an egg refers to its quality, not its age. The freshest eggs are Grade AA, followed by Grade A and Grade B. The color of the shell has no influence on egg quality.

Eggs are also classified according to size and weight, as outlined in the chart above.

When eggs are graded, the carton or case receives a label that indicates the grade (freshness) and size. Although quality and size are both marked on the carton, they are not interrelated—that is, the largest eggs are not necessarily of the best quality. Eggs of any size may be in any of the three grades.

Market Forms of Eggs

Fresh

Fresh or shell eggs are used most often in the foodservice operation.

Frozen

Frozen eggs are available in several forms:
▼ Whole eggs
▼ Whites
▼ Yolks
▼ Whole eggs with extra yolks

Frozen eggs are usually made from high-quality fresh eggs and are excellent for use in scrambled eggs, omelets, French toast, and baked goods. They are pasteurized and are usually purchased in 30-pound cans. Frozen eggs take at least 2 days to thaw at cooler temperatures.

Dried

Dried eggs are available in these forms:
▼ Whole
▼ Yolks
▼ Whites (albumen)

Dried eggs are used primarily for baking. They are not suggested for use in breakfast cookery. Unlike most dehydrated products, dried eggs are not shelf stable and must be kept refrigerated or frozen, tightly sealed.

Maintaining Quality and Storage

Proper storage is essential for maintaining quality. Eggs keep for weeks if held at 36°F, but they lose quality quickly if held at room temperature. In fact, they can lose a full grade in one day at warm kitchen temperatures. There's no point in paying for Grade AA eggs if they are Grade B by the time you use them.

Store eggs away from other foods that might pass on undesirable flavors or odors.

Nutritional Contributions of Eggs

The nutrients in eggs are so well balanced that they can be rated with milk as a nearly perfect food. Eggs make important contributions to nutritional needs. The yolk in particular is a rich source of nutrients and contains more vitamins and minerals than the white; it also contains some fat. However, yolk and white are most often used together, and thus the nutrient values are usually considered for the whole egg, not for the yolk or the white alone.

Protein

Eggs, like milk, contain complete protein, which is needed for growth and for repair of body tissues. Most of the protein is found in the whites. With their high-quality protein, eggs can be used as a substitute for meat.

Vitamins

The yolk contains most of the vitamins found in the egg. The egg white contains only riboflavin. The yolk contains vitamins A and D; it is a good source of vitamin B_2 and a fair source of vitamin B_1; and it contains a trace of niacin. Eggs are also an important source of vitamin D, a nutrient not found in most other common foods.

Minerals

The most important minerals provided by eggs are iron and phosphorus, found only in the yolk. Iron is not widely distributed in foods; in addition to eggs, it is found in meats and green leafy vegetables.

Iron is essential for the formation of hemoglobin, the red pigment of the blood. Hemoglobin carries oxygen to the cells and carries carbon dioxide away to be eliminated. When there are too few red blood cells, a condition called anemia develops. Because eggs are such an important source of iron and thus a booster of hemoglobin, they help prevent anemia.

Fat

Only the yolk contains fat. Vitamins A and D, because they are fat soluble, are dissolved in fat. The fat in egg yolk also helps to meet some of the body's energy needs.

The following chart details the nutritive value of an egg as compared to one slice of prepared beef.

Principles of Egg Cookery

The principles of egg cookery are very much influenced by the egg's high protein content. As with all protein, high temperatures and overcooking cause toughening. Whether eggs are

COMPARATIVE NUTRITIVE VALUE OF AN EGG		
	ONE COOKED EGG	ONE SLICE PREPARED BEEF
Protein (gm)	6.0	7.8
Calcium (mg)	25.0	3.0
Iron (mg)	1.3	1.0
Vitamin A (I.U.)	538	0
Thiamine (mg)	0.04	0.02
Ascorbic acid (mg)	0	0
Riboflavin (mg)	0.13	0.06

cooked alone or combined with other foods, you should observe these principles:

▼ Use low temperatures to prevent toughening, curdling, and discoloration.
▼ Cook only until desired firmness is achieved.

Functions of Eggs in Cookery

Eggs serve many important functions in cookery and are used in a variety of foods. Because of their color, flavor, viscosity, and ability to coagulate, eggs are valuable in various food preparation processes. They may be prepared alone or combined with other foods. Either way they will enhance the nutritional value of the prepared food and the meal.

Following are the functions of eggs in cookery:

▼ To add nutrients. This is one of the most important functions of eggs because of their high nutrient content.
▼ To improve color, flavor, and texture of food products. Most foods look and taste better when eggs are added. Eggs used in puddings, custards, and ice creams improve their color, flavor, and texture. In baked foods, eggs will improve the browning of the outer crust and give a creamy or yellow color to the interior.
▼ To thicken liquids and bind food together or coat foods for frying. When eggs are heated, the protein will coagulate and

become firm, with a tender texture. (However, if the heating is too prolonged or if the temperature is too high, the protein in egg—like all protein—will overcoagulate and become tough and rubbery.)

▼ The protein in both the egg white and the yolk is a thickening agent. Because of the ability of this protein to coagulate or clot, eggs can be used to thicken food mixtures when heated. The coagulated egg will be firm. The coagulation process will thicken custards, help to form the outer shells of cream puffs and the cell walls of cakes, bind together the ingredients of meat loaves, and hold crumbs together for coating on breaded food.

▼ To act as leavening agent. The leavening action of eggs is due to the air that can be beaten into the white. Beaten egg white can form a foam that holds a large quantity of air. The air bubbles in the foam are surrounded by a film of egg white. When the foam is heated the air bubbles expand, the egg white stretches, and then the egg coagulates to give a light, porous structure to the product. The yolk forms only a small amount of foam and is not used for leavening.

▼ To act as emulsifying agent. The egg yolk has emulsifying properties because its proteins can surround tiny globules of oil and keep them from separating. Eggs act as an emulsifying agent in many foods including cakes, popovers, and mayonnaise.

The many functions of eggs in food preparation are highlighted in Figure 18-2.

Preparation and Uses of Eggs in Cookery

During cooking eggs coagulate, with the degree of coagulation dependent on the cooking temperature and length of cooking time. Eggs may coagulate only slightly, as in soft-cooked eggs, or more completely, as in hard-cooked eggs.

Eggs may be cooked in the shell or out of the shell (for example, fried or poached), and they are an ingredient in many dishes. Remember, when eggs are cooked alone or in combination with other foods, the best results are obtained when temperatures are low and time is carefully controlled to give the desired degree of firmness.

When eggs are used alone or as the principal ingredient, it is important to use eggs of high quality.

Procedures for Cooking Eggs

Because eggs are used in many different preparations, as well as, for a stand-alone ertrée, it is vital to follow procedures carefully.

Eggs Cooked in the Shell

1. Assemble equipment and food items.
2. Bring eggs to room temperature: Remove them from the cooler 1 hour before cooking; or place them in warm water for 5 minutes, and drain. This step is necessary because cold eggs are more likely to crack when placed in boiling water.

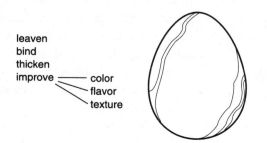

leaven
bind
thicken
improve —— color
        —— flavor
        —— texture

Eggs Can:

Leaven	(sponge cakes)
Emulsify	(mayonnaise)
Bind	(meat loaf)
Thicken	(custard)
Structure	(popovers and pastry shells)

FIGURE 18-2   The Versatile Egg

3. Place eggs in boiling water, and return the water to a simmer.
4. Simmer (do not boil) for the required time:
   — Soft-cooked eggs—3 to 4 minutes
   — Medium-cooked eggs—5 to 7 minutes
   — Hard-cooked eggs—12 to 15 minutes
   Exact cooking time depends on the temperature and size of the eggs and the amount of water used.
5. Drain immediately and cool under cold running water to stop the cooking. Cool just a few seconds if eggs are to be served hot. Cool further if they are to be held for later use. Ice baths are appropriate in some cases.
6. To peel, crack the shell and pull it away, starting at the large end (where the air cell is located). For easier peeling, peel while still warm, and hold under running water to help loosen the shell.

Very fresh eggs are hard to peel. Eggs for cooking in the shell should be several days old. Following are the standards of quality for hard-cooked eggs:

▼ Evenly coagulated whites and yolks
▼ Whites glossy and firm but tender; not tough or rubbery
▼ No dark color on outside of yolk
▼ Pleasing flavor

Poached Eggs

1. Assemble equipment and food items.
2. Use the freshest Grade AA eggs, whenever possible, for best results. These maintain their shape best because yolks and whites are firm.
3. If eggs are not very fresh, add 1 teaspoon salt and 2 teaspoons distilled vinegar per quart of water. The vinegar speeds coagulation of the egg white so that it will keep its shape better. Do not add vinegar if very fresh eggs are used because it will make whites tougher and less shiny.
4. Bring water just to a simmer. If the water is boiling, eggs will toughen and may break

up with the agitation. If the water is not hot enough, eggs will not cook quickly enough and will spread.
5. Break eggs one at a time into a dish or a small plate, and slide them into the simmering water. Eggs will hold their shape better if they slide in against the edge of the pan.
6. Simmer 3 to 5 minutes, until whites are coagulated and yolks are still soft.
7. Remove the eggs from the pan with a slotted spoon or skimmer.
8. To serve immediately, drain very well. For a better appearance, trim off the ragged edges.
9. To hold for later service, plunge eggs immediately into cold water to stop the cooking. At service time, reheat briefly in hot water.

Following are the standards of quality for poached eggs:

▼ Bright, shiny appearance
▼ Compact, round shape, not spread or flattened
▼ Firm but tender whites; warm, liquid yolks

Eggs Fried to Order

1. Assemble all equipment and food items. Eggs may be fried in small, individual sauté pans or on the griddle. Griddled eggs are not as attractive because they tend to spread more.
2. Select very fresh, Grade AA eggs for best results.
3. Add about ⅛ inch of fat to the sauté pan and set it over moderate heat, or preheat the griddle to 325°F and ladle on a small quantity of fat. Too much fat will make the eggs greasy; too little will cause them to stick.
4. Break the eggs in a dish. This lessens the chance of breaking the yolks.
5. When the fat is hot enough that a drop of water sizzles when dropped into it, slide the eggs into the pan (or onto the griddle). If the fat is not hot enough, the eggs will

spread too much and may stick. If it is too hot, the eggs will become tough or even crisp.

6. Reduce heat to low (if using sauté pan) and cook the eggs to order as follows:
Sunnyside up. Cook slowly without flipping until white is completely set and yolk is still soft and yellow. Heat must be low, or bottom will toughen or burn before top is completely set.
Basted. Do not flip. Add a few drops of water to pan and cover so steam cooks the top. Yolk will have a thin film of coagulated white covering it. Yolk should remain liquid.
Over easy. Fry and flip over. Cook until white is set and yolk is still liquid.
Over medium. Fry and flip over. Cook just until yolk is partially set.
Over hard. Fry and flip over. Cook until yolk is completely set.

Following are the standards of quality for fried eggs:

▼ Whites shiny, uniformly set, and tender—not browned, blistered, or crisp at edges
▼ Yolks set properly according to desired doneness (Sunnyside-up yolks should be yellow and well rounded. In other styles, the yolk is covered with a thin layer of coagulated white.)
▼ Final product relatively compact, standing high, not spread out and thin

Scrambled Eggs

1. Assemble all equipment and food items.
2. Break eggs into a stainless steel bowl and beat until well blended. Season with salt and white pepper. **Do not use aluminum, which may discolor the eggs.**
3. If desired, add a small amount of milk, cream, or water—about 1 to 1½ tablespoons for two eggs, or 8 to 12 ounces per quart of eggs. Too much liquid tends to make cooked eggs watery and dilute the flavor. Heavy cream adds richness but also adds cost.

4. Heat butter in a small sauté pan (for cooking to order) or in a large skillet, as for fried eggs.
5. When fat is just hot enough to make a drop of water sizzle, pour in eggs.
6. Cook over low heat, stirring gently from time to time as the eggs coagulate. Lift portions of the coagulated egg so that the uncooked egg can run underneath. Too much stirring breaks up eggs into very small particles.
7. Do not let the eggs brown. Keep heat low.
8. When eggs are set but still soft and moist, remove from the heat. Turn out onto plate or into steam table pan.

Omelets

1. Assemble all equipment and ingredients.
2. Beat two or three eggs in a small bowl just until well mixed. Do not whip until frothy. Season with salt and pepper.
3. Place an omelet pan over high heat.
4. When the pan is hot, add about 1 tablespoon clarified butter and swirl it around to coat the inside of the pan. Give it a second to get hot. **Raw butter may be used, but great care is necessary to keep it from burning.**
5. Add the eggs to the pan. They should begin to coagulate around the edges and on the bottom in a few seconds.
6. With one hand vigorously shake the pan back and forth. At the same time, stir the eggs in a circular motion with the bottom side of a fork, but do not let the fork scrape the pan.
7. Stop shaking and stirring when the eggs are almost set but still very moist. If you continue stirring, you will have scrambled eggs instead of an omelet.
8. Tilt the handle up and shake the pan so that the omelet slides to the opposite side of the pan and begins to climb up the opposite slope.
9. For a filled omelet, spoon the filling across the center of the egg, at right angles to the handle.

10. With a fork, fold the sides of the omelet over the center. The omelet should be approximately oval and be resting in the center of the pan.

11. Grasp the handle of the pan with your palm underneath and tilt the omelet out onto a plate so that it inverts and keeps an oval shape.

Egg Foo Yong

Yield: 4 servings

INGREDIENTS NEEDED

1 c finely diced cooked ham,
roast pork, or chicken
1 c drained canned bean sprouts
¾ c chopped onion
1 tbsp soy sauce
½ tsp salt (omit if using ham)
6 eggs, beaten slightly
2 tbsp vegetable oil

EQUIPMENT NEEDED

Cutting board
Liquid and dry measures
Sauté pan or heavy skillet
French knife
Wire whip

PROCEDURE

1. Mix meat, bean sprouts, onion, soy sauce, and salt. Stir in eggs.
2. Heat oil in skillet or sauté pan. Drop a fourth of mixture into hot fat to form a patty. Cook about 5 minutes or until browned on one side; turn and brown other side.
3. Remove patty from skillet; drain well. Transfer to a warm heat-resistant platter; keep warm in a 200°F oven while cooking remaining patties.

Cheese Soufflé

Yield: 8 to 10 servings

INGREDIENTS NEEDED

½ lb sharp cheddar cheese
6 tbsp butter or margarine
6 tbsp all-purpose flour
¾ tsp dry mustard
½ tsp salt
⅛ tsp white pepper
⅛ tsp paprika
1½ c milk
6 egg yolks
6 egg whites

EQUIPMENT NEEDED

Cutting board
Grater
2-qt casserole dish
Liquid and dry measures
Wire whip
Saucepan
Spoon
2 small bowls
Oven, preheated to 300°F

PROCEDURE

1. Set out 2-quart casserole; do not grease.
2. Grate cheese and set aside.
3. Melt butter or margarine in saucepan over low heat.
4. Blend in flour, dry mustard, salt, white pepper, and paprika.
5. Heat until mixture bubbles. Remove from heat. Add milk **gradually** while stirring constantly.
6. Return to heat and bring rapidly to boiling, **stirring constantly;** cook 1 to 2 minutes longer. Cool slightly, and add grated cheese all at one time. Stir rapidly until cheese is melted.
7. Beat egg yolks until thick and lemon colored.
8. Slowly spoon cheese sauce into egg yolks **while stirring vigorously.**
9. Beat egg whites until rounded peaks are formed and whites do not slide when the bowl is partially inverted.
10. Gently spread egg yolk mixture over beaten egg whites. Carefully fold together until just blended. Turn mixture into casserole. Insert tip of spoon 1 inch deep into the mixture, 1 to 1½ inches from edge; run a line around mixture.
11. Bake at 300°F 1 to 1¼ hours, or until a silver knife comes out clean when inserted halfway between center and the edge of soufflé.
12. Serve at once, while "top hat" is at its height.

Puffy Cheese Omelet

Yield: 3 servings

INGREDIENTS NEEDED

4 oz cheddar cheese (about 1 c grated)
2 tbsp butter or margarine
3 egg whites
3 tbsp water
½ tsp salt
Few grains white pepper
3 egg yolks

EQUIPMENT NEEDED

Liquid and dry measures
10-in. heavy skillet
Grater
Wire whip
Rubber spatula
Metal spatula
Oven, preheated to 350°F

PROCEDURE

1. Grate cheese and set aside.
2. Heat skillet until just hot enough to sizzle a drop of water. Heat butter or margarine in skillet.
3. Meanwhile, beat egg whites until frothy.
4. Add water, salt, and white pepper to egg whites.
5. Continue beating until rounded peaks are formed. (Beaten egg whites should stand no longer than it takes to beat yolks.)
6. Beat egg yolks until thick and lemon colored.
7. Spread egg yolks over whites and gently fold together.
8. Turn egg mixture into skillet. Level surface gently. Cook ½ minute on top of range; lower heat and cook slowly about 10 minutes, or until lightly browned on bottom and puffy but still moist on top. Do not stir at any time.
9. Place skillet with omelet in a 350°F oven about 5 minutes. Remove and sprinkle all grated cheese over top. Return to oven and continue baking until cheese is melted.
10. To serve, loosen edges with metal spatula; make a quick, shallow cut through center; and fold one side over. Gently slip omelet onto a warm serving platter. Or omit shallow cut and folding and, using two forks, tear omelet gently into wedges. Invert wedges on warm serving dish so browned side is on top.

Eggs Florentine à l'Orange

Yield: 4 servings

INGREDIENTS NEEDED
1 tbsp butter or margarine
½ c onion, chopped
¼ lb mushrooms, cleaned and sliced
1 package (10 oz) frozen chopped spinach, thawed and drained
1 tsp salt
⅛ tsp pepper
*1 cup orange sections**
4 eggs

EQUIPMENT NEEDED
Cutting board
Liquid and dry measures
French knife
Paring knife
4 ramekins
Medium saucepan
Oven, preheated to 350°F

PROCEDURE

1. Melt butter or margarine in saucepan. Add onions and cook until tender; add mushrooms and cook 5 minutes. Stir in spinach, salt, pepper, and orange sections.
2. Divide equally among 4 buttered ramekins, making a depression in center of each.
3. Bake in a 350°F oven 15 to 20 minutes or until hot.
4. Add 1 egg to depression in each dish; sprinkle with additional salt and pepper. Bake 7 to 10 minutes longer, or until egg white is set.

*To section oranges, cut off peel round and round spiral fashion. Go over fruit again, removing any remaining white membrane. Cut along side of each dividing membrane from outside to middle of core. Remove section by section over a bowl; reserve juice for other use.

French Omelet

Yield: 4 to 6 servings

INGREDIENTS NEEDED
6 eggs
6 tbsp milk or water
¾ tsp salt
⅛ tsp black pepper
3 tbsp butter or margarine

EQUIPMENT NEEDED
Liquid and dry measures
Wire whip
10-in. heavy skillet
Spoon
Metal spatula

PROCEDURE

1. Beat eggs, milk, salt, and pepper together until well blended.
2. Heat skillet until just hot enough to sizzle a drop of water; melt butter in skillet.
3. Pour egg mixture into skillet. As edges of the omelet begin to thicken, draw cooked portions toward center with a spoon or fork to allow uncooked mixture to flow to bottom of skillet, tilting it as necessary; **do not stir.**
4. When eggs are thickened but surface is still moist, increase heat to brown bottom of omelet quickly. Loosen edges carefully and fold in half; slide onto a warm serving platter. If desired, garnish with sprigs of parsley.

Eggs Benedict

Yield: 2 portions

INGREDIENTS NEEDED
1 English muffin
2 eggs
2 2-oz slices Canadian bacon
1½ oz hollandaise sauce

EQUIPMENT NEEDED
Liquid measures
Metal spatula
Ladle (1½ oz)
Sauté pan

PROCEDURE

1. Toast muffin (one half for each order). Spread with butter and place on serving plate.
2. Poach egg according to basic procedure given earlier in text.
3. While egg is poaching, heat Canadian bacon for one minute in a sauté pan. Place meat on top of toasted muffin.
4. Drain poached egg well and place it on top of Canadian bacon.
5. Ladle hollandaise sauce over top. Serve immediately.

PRODUCT EVALUATION SHEET

Name _____   Lab date _____

Product prepared _____   Total prep time _____

Cooking method _____

Describe the following in one or two short sentences.

APPEARANCE (size, shape, consistency, etc.):

COLOR (golden brown, pasty white, bright, dull, etc.):

TEXTURE (smooth, lumpy, fine, coarse, sticky, gummy, etc.):

FLAVOR (sweet, sour, bitter, strong, spicy, bland, etc.):

TEMPERATURE (warm, hot, cold . . . Is it appropriate for the product?):

PROBLEMS ENCOUNTERED:

SOLUTION:
Suggestions to alter or improve the product:
1.

2.

Rating (10 being perfect):

0   1   2   3   4   5   6   7   8   9   10

19

Salads

Parts of a Salad

Any successful salad will contain four basic parts: base, body, dressing, and garnish. Each part is extremely important in salad preparation. If just one part is omitted or done poorly, the finished product will suffer.

Base

The **base** usually consists of a salad green such as leaf, romaine, head, or Bibb lettuce. It can be eaten, but in most cases guests will choose to leave it on the plate or in the bowl. The main purpose of the base is to keep the plate or bowl from looking bare and to provide color contrast to the body.

Body

The **body** is the main part of the salad, the part that should be given the most attention. The type of salad determines the kind or kinds of ingredients used. The body should be prepared by the rules of good salad preparation.

Dressing

A **dressing** is usually served with every type of salad. It adds flavor, provides food value, helps digestion, improves palatability, and in some cases acts as a garnish.

Garnish

The main purpose of the **garnish** is to add eye appeal to the finished product, but in some cases it may even improve the form or enhance the taste. The garnish may be a part of the basic salad ingredients, or it may be an additional item that will blend with and complement the body.

The garnish should be simple. It should attract the diner's attention without being distracting, and it should help stimulate the appetite.

Types of Salads

Salads may by grouped according to the foods from which they are made or according to the way they are used in a meal. The following salad groupings reflect different categories of main ingredients: green, fruit, poultry, egg, vegetable, meat, fish, and gelatin. The following groupings reflect different uses within the meal: accompaniment, appetizer, entrée, and dessert.

Accompaniment Salads

Salads are most frequently used as an accompaniment to a main course of meat, poultry, fish, or a casserole. These are light, small salads that stimulate the appetite. Salad greens, tart fruits, and combinations of raw vegetables may be used in tossed salads, for example.

You may prefer to use raw fruits and vegetables in your salads because of their crisp texture. However, cooked or canned fruits and vegetables offer variety and make suitable accompaniment salads. Other possibilities include gelatin salads with fruits or vegetables added.

Entrée and Combination Salads

Cold salads have become very popular on luncheon menus, especially among nutrition- and diet-conscious diners. The appeal of these salads is in their variety and freshness of ingredients.

▼ Entrée salads should be large enough to serve as a full meal and should contain a substantial portion of protein. Meat, poultry, and seafood salads, as well as egg salad and cheese, are popular choices.

▼ Entrée salads should offer enough variety on the plate to constitute a balanced meal, both nutritionally and in terms of flavor and texture. In addition to the protein, a salad platter should offer a variety of vegetables, greens, and/or fruits. Examples are chef's salad (mixed greens, raw vegetables, and strips of meat and cheese), shrimp or crabmeat salad with tomato wedges and slices of avocado on a bed of greens, and cottage cheese with an assortment of fruits.

▼ The portion size and variety of ingredients give the chef an excellent opportunity to apply imagination and creativity to produce attractive, appetizing salad plates. Attractive arrangements and good color balance are important.

Fruit Salads

A fruit salad is any salad in which fruit predominates. It is generally composed of cut or sectioned fruit, served separately or combined. Berries of many varieties are sometimes added to enhance flavor and add color.

The handling of fruits for salads requires some special product knowledge and techniques. Certain fresh fruits—apples, pears, peaches, bananas, and avocados—discolor when exposed to air. Like lettuce, they must be cut with stainless steel cutting edges. If you combine such fruits with citrus fruits, the high acid content of the latter prevents the rapid discoloration of the fruits that are vulnerable to air. Alternatively, you can rinse vulnerable fruits in lemon juice and water or an ascorbic acid solution, though this does compromise the flavor.

Fruits that are peeled should be washed as close as possible to use time. Berries in particular, especially strawberries and raspberries, do not hold well. Wash them just before use, drain them well, and add them just before service.

Many canned fruits are good salad material—mandarin oranges, peaches, pears, apricots, grapefruit, pineapple, and sweet cherries. Drain them carefully, or they will make for a watery plate. Dried fruits—for instance, dates and prunes—are also used.

Almost all fruits may be combined. Flavor, color, variety, and availability will determine choices.

Other foods may be added to a fruit salad to spark flavor or texture. For example, the famous Waldorf salad combines diced apples and celery with chopped walnuts. Those ingredients are mixed with a mayonnaise or chantilly dressing, which holds the salad together.

Fruit salads are usually, but not always, served on lettuce. They are usually accompanied by a dressing (sometimes a sweet one), but by no means always.

Congealed Salads

A congealed salad is any salad that contains gelatin that holds it together. Gelatin comes in three primary forms:

▼ **Clear or unflavored gelatin** comes in two principal forms—powder and leaves. The leaves look like heavy plastic film. Good-quality powdered gelatin has a softness and sheen referred to as **bloom.**

▼ **Fruit-flavored gelatin** comes in powdered form in assorted flavors under many familiar brand names. It contains sugar as well as color and flavor.

▼ **Aspic** is a powdered meat-flavored gelatin. It is usually beef flavored, but it also comes in fish and poultry flavors.

There are two methods of handling gelatin, one for clear gelatin and the other for fruit-flavored gelatin and aspic. For clear gelatin, the first step is to mix it with cold water. Then stir the mixture into boiling hot water, dissolve it completely, and cool. Dispersing the gelatin in cold water first will keep it from lumping. Then, dissolving it in boiling hot water, as many product labels advise, will give you the best end results. (Technically, gelatin will dissolve at 100°F, but it will take a very long time.) For aspic and fruit-flavored gelatin, only one step is necessary: Dissolve the powder in very hot water, then cool.

The end product for all gelatins is a jellied substance that forms when the mixture is cold. **It is important to get the right proportion of liquid to gelatin.** Too much liquid will make the gel wobbly; too little will make it rubbery. You can substitute fruit juice or another suitable liquid for part or all of the water.

Many different fruits, vegetables, and other foods can be added to gelatin as it begins to jell. Drain them well so that the proportion of liquid to gelatin does not change and spoil the consistency. You can add almost any fruit or vegetable. **The few exceptions are pineapple, figs, and papaya.** These fruits contain certain enzymes that keep the gelatin from congealing. However, the same fruits cooked or canned cause no trouble.

Salad Ingredients

Freshness and variety of ingredients are essential for quality salads. Lettuce, of course, is the first choice for most people; but many other foods can make up a salad. Lettuce or some other leafy vegetable is present in the majority of salads. Following are descriptions of a wide variety of salad greens:

Iceberg lettuce. The most popular salad ingredient. Firm, compact head with crisp, mild-tasting pale green leaves. Valuable for its texture because it stays crisp longer than other lettuces. Can be used alone but is best mixed with more flavorful greens such as romaine because it lacks flavor itself. Keeps well.

Romaine or coss lettuce. Essential for Caesar salads. Elongated, loosely packed head with dark green, coarse leaves. Crisp texture; full, sweet flavor. Keeps well and is easy to handle. For elegant service, the center rib is often removed.

Boston lettuce. With cup-shaped leaves, excellent for salad bases. Small, round heads with soft, fragile leaves. Deep green outside, shading to nearly white inside. The leaves have a rich, mild flavor and delicate, buttery texture. Bruises easily and does not keep well.

Bibb or limestone lettuce. Similar to Boston lettuce but smaller and more delicate. A whole head may be only a few inches across. Color ranges from dark green outside to creamy yellow at the core. Tenderness, delicate flavor, and high price make it a luxury in some markets. The small, whole leaves are often served by themselves, with a light vinaigrette dressing, as an after-dinner salad.

Loose-leaf lettuce. Forms bunches rather than heads. Soft, fragile leaves with curly edges. May be all green or with shades of red. Wilts easily and does not keep well, but is inexpensive and gives flavor, variety, and interest to mixed salad greens.

Escarole or Broad-leaf endive. Coarse-textured and slightly tough, with somewhat bitter flavor. Broad, thick leaves in bunches rather than heads. Mix with sweeter greens to vary flavor and texture, but do not use alone because of bitterness. Escarole is frequently braised with olive oil and garlic and served as a vegetable in Italian cuisine.

Chicory or curly endive. Narrow, curly, twisted leaves with firm texture and bitter flavor. Outside leaves are dark green; core is yellow or white. Attractive when mixed with other greens or used as a base or garnish but too bitter to be used alone.

Belgian endive or witloof chicory. Crisp leaves with waxy texture and pleasantly bitter flavor. Narrow, lightly packed, pointed heads resembling spearheads, 4 to 6 inches long. Pale yel-

POPULAR SALAD INGREDIENTS

SALAD GREENS	RAW VEGETABLES	PREPARED VEGETABLES	STARCHES	FRUITS
Iceberg	Cabbage	Artichoke hearts	Dried beans	Apples
Romaine	Carrots	Asparagus	Potatoes	Apricots
Boston	Cauliflower	Beans (all kinds)	Macaroni products	Avocados
Bibb	Celery	Beets	Rice	Bananas
Loose-leaf	Cucumbers	Carrots	Bread (croutons)	Berries
Escarole	Kohlrabi	Cauliflower		Cherries
Chicory	Mushrooms	Pickles		Coconut
Curly endive	Onions	Hearts of palm		Dates
Belgian endive	Scallions	Leeks		Figs
Chinese cabbage	Red peppers	Olives		Grapes
Spinach	Green peppers	Peas		Grapefruit
Watercress	Radishes	Roasted peppers		Kiwi
Dandelion greens	Tomatoes	Pimentos		Mangos
		Potatoes		Melons
		Water chestnuts		Oranges
				Papayas
				Peaches
				Pears
				Pineapple
				Raisins

low-green to white in color. Usually very expensive. Often served alone, split in half or into wedges, or separated into leaves, accompanied by a mustard vinaigrette dressing.

Chinese cabbage or celery cabbage. Adds excellent flavor to mixed salad greens. Elongated, light green heads with broad white center ribs. Tender but crisp, with mild cabbage flavor. Also used extensively in Chinese cooking.

Spinach. Excellent salad greens when leaves are small and tender. Used either alone or mixed with other greens. A very popular salad is spinach leaves garnished with sliced, raw mushrooms and crisp, crumbled bacon. Spinach must be washed very thoroughly, and the coarse stems must be removed.

Watercress. Most commonly used as a garnish; also excellent in salads. Small, dark green, oval leaves with a pungent, peppery flavor. Remove thick stems before adding to salads.

Dandelion greens. The familiar lawn plant also cultivated for use in the kitchen. Only young, tender leaves must be used. Older leaves are coarse and bitter, though cultivated varieties are milder than wild dandelion. The best greens are picked in the spring.

The above chart lists, by category, most of the ingredients used in popular American salads. You will think of others. Add them to the category lists as they occur to you or as they are suggested to you by your instructors. The lists will be useful to you when you are creating your own salad ideas.

Nutritional Contributions of Salads

The nutritional value of a salad is determined by the ingredients used to make it. Fresh fruits and vegetables are important sources of vitamins, minerals, and cellulose. Dark leafy greens are especially helpful in meeting the body's needs for iron and for vitamins A and C.

When you make whole salads from greens, the salad can be counted as one serving of a leafy vegetable. The green leaf that you use as a base for a salad is too small to be counted as a serving.

Other foods commonly used in salads include meat, fish, poultry, cheese, and egg, all rich sources of complete protein. Nuts and mature beans contribute only incomplete proteins.

The caloric value of salads, in general, is relatively low. The starchy vegetables such as potatoes and mature beans, as well as cereal products such as macaroni, are higher in calories than fruits and succulent vegetables. Potato and macaroni salads contain starch and help meet the body's energy needs.

Salads not only provide appetizing and interesting ways to serve fresh fruits and vegetables but also add texture to meals and contribute important nutrients. The value of these nutrients should be preserved.

Principles of Salad Preparation

Most salads are made in quantity, so an assembly line production system is most efficient. There is little cooking involved, but there is a great deal of time-consuming handwork. Salads can be made quickly and efficiently only if the station is set up properly. Thorough **prepreparation** is extremely important.

Here are some principles that will streamline your salad preparation:

1. Prepare all ingredients. Wash and cut greens. Prepare cooked vegetables. Cut all fruits, vegetables, and garnishes. Mix bound and marinated salads (egg salad, potato salad, three-bean salad, etc.). Have all ingredients chilled.
2. Arrange salad plates on work tables. Line them up on trays for easy transferring to cooler.
3. Place bases or underliners on all plates.
4. Arrange body of salad on all plates.
5. Garnish all salads.
6. Refrigerate until service. Do not hold more than a few hours or salads will wilt. Holding boxes should have high humidity.
7. Do not add dressing to green salads until service, or they will wilt.

Figure 19-1 will give you some ideas for salad presentation.

Procedures for Salad Preparation

In salad preparation you will enjoy using your imagination and creative talents.

Green Salads

1. Wash greens thoroughly. Remove the core from head lettuce by striking it gently against the side of the sink and twisting it out. (Do not smash it, or you'll bruise the entire head.) Cut through the cores of other greens, or separate the leaves so that all traces of grit can be removed. Wash in several changes of cold water until completely clean. For iceberg lettuce, run cold water into the core end (after removing core), and then invert to drain.
2. Drain greens well. Lift greens from the water and drain in a colander. Tools and machines are available to spin-dry greens quickly. Poor draining results in a watered-down dressing and a soupy, soggy salad.
3. Crisp the greens. Refrigerate them in a colander covered with damp towels or in a perforated storage bin to allow air circulation and complete drainage.

FIGURE 19-1 Salad Presentation

4. Cut or tear into bite-size pieces. Many people insist on tearing leaves instead of cutting, but this is a very slow method if you are working with a large quantity. Also, you are more likely to crush or bruise the leaves. Use sharp stainless steel knives for cutting. Bite-size pieces are important as a convenience to the customer—it is difficult to eat or cut large leaves with a salad fork.

5. Mix the greens. Toss gently until uniformly mixed. Nonjuicy raw vegetable garnish such as green pepper strips or carrot shreds may be mixed in at this time. Just make sure the vegetables are not cut into compact little chunks that will settle to the bottom of the bowl. Broad, thin slices or shreds stay better mixed.

6. Plate the salads. Always use cold plates. **Never use plates right from the dishwasher.** Avoid plating salads more than an hour or two before service, or they are likely to wilt or dry.

7. Add garnish. Exceptions:

— Garnish that is tossed with the greens in step 5.

— Garnish that will not hold well (croutons will get soggy, avocado will discolor, etc.). Add these at service time.

8. Refrigerate until service.

9. Add dressing immediately before service, or serve it on the side. **Dressed greens will wilt rapidly.**

Fruit Salads

1. Fruit salads are often arranged rather than mixed or tossed because most fruits are delicate and easily broken. An exception is the Waldorf salad, made of firm apples mixed with nuts, celery, and mayonnaise-based dressing.

2. Place broken or less attractive pieces of fruit on the bottom of the salad, with the more attractive pieces arranged on top.

3. Some fruits, such as apples and bananas, discolor when cut and should be dipped into an acid such as tart fruit juice.

4. Fruits do not hold as well as vegetables after being cut. If you are preparing both vegetable and fruit salads for a particular meal service, the vegetable salads should usually be prepared first.

5. Drain canned fruits well before including them in the salad, or the salad will be watery and sloppy. The liquid may be reserved for use in fruit salad dressings or other preparations.

Vegetable Salads

1. Neat, accurate cutting of ingredients is important because the shapes of the vegetables add to eye appeal. The design or arrangement of a vegetable salad is often based on variety in shapes, such as long, slender asparagus stalks and green beans, tomato wedges, cucumber slices, green pepper strips or rings, and radish flowers.

2. Cut vegetables as close as possible to serving time, or they may dry or shrivel at the edges.

3. Cooked vegetables should have firm, crisp texture and good color. Mushy, overcooked vegetables are unattractive in a salad.

4. After cooking, vegetables must be thoroughly drained and well chilled before being included in the salad.

5. Vegetables are sometimes marinated, or soaked in a seasoned liquid, before being made into salads, as in three-bean salad or mushrooms à la Grecque. The marinade is usually some form of oil and vinegar dressing, which also serves as the dressing for the salad. **Do not plate marinated salads too far ahead of time, or the lettuce base will wilt.** Use crisp, sturdy greens (such as iceberg, romaine, or chicory) as bases because they do not wilt as quickly.

Cooked Salads

1. Cool cooked ingredients thoroughly before mixing them with mayonnaise, and **keep the completed salad mixture chilled at all times.** Mayonnaise-type salads are ideal breeding grounds for bacteria that cause food poisoning.

2. Cooked salads are good ways to use leftovers such as chicken, meat, or fish, but **the meat ingredient must have been handled according to the rules of good sanitation.** The product will not be cooked again to destroy any bacteria that might grow in the salad and cause illness.

3. To preserve nutrients, cook potatoes for salads whole, then peel and cut them.

4. Don't cut ingredients too small, or the final product will be like mush or paste, with no textural interest.

5. Crisp vegetables are usually added for texture. Celery is the most popular, but other choices might be green peppers, carrots, chopped pickles, onions, water chestnuts, or apples. Be sure that flavors harmonize, however.

6. Bland main ingredients, such as potatoes or some seafoods, may be marinated in a seasoned liquid such as vinaigrette before being mixed with the mayonnaise and other ingredients. First drain any marinade not absorbed to avoid thinning out the mayonnaise.

7. Fold in thick dressing gently to avoid crushing or breaking the main ingredients.

8. Bound salads are usually portioned with a scoop. This procedure has two advantages: It provides portion control, and it gives height and shape to the salad.

9. Choose attractive, colorful garnishes. A scoop of potato or chicken salad looks pretty pale and uninteresting without a garnish.

Gelatin Salads

1. Use the right amount of gelatin for the volume of liquid in the recipe. Too much gelatin makes a stiff, rubbery product; too little will result in a product that will not hold its shape.

   Basic proportions for **unflavored gelatin** are 2½ ounces dry gelatin per gal-

SALAD TERMS

Appetizer salad: A salad served before a meal

Base: The bottom layer of a salad

Body: The part of a salad that contains the main ingredient; often gives the salad its name

Core: The center of a head of lettuce or a piece of fruit

Crispness: Crunchy, fresh texture or condition of greens

Dessert salad: A light, usually sweet salad served after a meal

Dressing: A liquid or semiliquid sauce for salads

Durable greens: Greens that do not bruise easily

Entrée salad: A large salad served as the main course of a meal

Fragile greens: Delicate greens that bruise easily

Garnish: A small, colorful piece of food that is placed on a salad for contrast of color, texture, and taste

Gelatin: A thickening agent used to make molded salads

Greens: Leafy green vegetables

Julienne: To cut into long thin strips

Mise en place: Setup, in place, of all ingredients, materials, and utensils needed for the preparation of a certain food

Rust: A reddish color that forms on greens that have been bruised

Salad: A combination of cooked or uncooked foods served cold with a dressing

Side salad: A salad that is served with an entrée and complements the taste and texture of the entrée

Wilted: Limp or droopy condition of greens

FRUIT TERMS

Ascorbic acid: A substance used to prevent cut fruits from discoloring

Citrus: The name of the fruit group to which oranges, grapefruit, lemons, and limes belong

Core: The central, seed-containing part of certain fruits

Hull: To remove the stems and leaves from berries

Membrane: The tough, thin layer of skin separating the segments of citrus fruits

Parisienne: A melon baller

Pit: A stonelike plant seed

Poach: To simmer briefly in slightly bubbling liquid

Prunes: Dried plums

Raisins: Dried grapes

Tropical fruits: Fruits grown in a warm climate

---

lon of liquid, but you will almost always need more than this because of acids and other ingredients in the recipe. Basic proportions for **sweetened, flavored gelatin** are 24 ounces per gallon of liquid.

Acids, such as fruit juices and vinegar, weaken the gelatin set, so when they are present you will need a higher proportion of gelatin, sometimes as much as 4 ounces or more per gallon. The setting power is also weakened if you whip the product into a foam or add a large quantity of chopped foods. Because the exact amount of gelatin needed varies with each recipe, test each recipe before using it.

2. Dissolve the gelatin in liquid. To dissolve **unflavored gelatin,** stir it into cold liquid to avoid lumping, and let it stand for 5 minutes to absorb water. Then heat it until dissolved, or add hot liquid and stir until dissolved. To dissolve **sweetened, flavored gelatin,** stir it into boiling water. It will not lump because the gelatin granules are held apart by sugar granules, much as starch granules in flour are held separate by the fat in a roux.

   To speed setting, dissolve the gelatin in up to half of the liquid, and add the remainder cold to lower temperature. For even faster setting, add crushed ice in place of an equal weight of cold water. Stir until melted.

3. Add solid ingredients when the gelatin is partially set—very thick and syrupy. This

will help keep them evenly mixed rather than floating or settling. Canned fruits or juicy items must be well drained before being added, or they will dilute the gelatin and weaken it.

Do not add raw pineapple or papaya to gelatin salads. They contain enzymes that dissolve the gelatin. If cooked or canned, however, these fruits may be added.

4. Pour gelatin into pans or individual molds, and refrigerate.

5. Prepare salad for service. Cut into equal portions if in a large pan, or unmold as follows:
   — Run a thin knife blade around the top edge of the mold to loosen.
   — Dip the mold into hot water for 1 or 2 seconds. Do not hold it there longer, or the gelatin will begin to melt.
   — Quickly wipe the bottom of the mold, and turn it over onto the salad plate (or invert the salad plate over the mold and flip the plate and mold over together).
   — If the gelatin doesn't unmold after a gentle shake, repeat the procedure. You may also wrap a towel, dipped in hot water and wrung out, around the mold until it releases, but this is more time-consuming.

6. Refrigerate gelatin salads until service to keep them firm.

Salade Niçoise

Yield: 6 to 8 servings

INGREDIENTS NEEDED

Dressing

½ c salad oil
1 tsp salt
½ tsp pepper
1 tsp dry mustard
1 tbsp parsley, finely chopped
1 tbsp chives, finely chopped
2 tbsp red wine vinegar

Salad

3 medium potatoes, cooked and sliced
9 oz frozen green beans, cooked
1 clove garlic, cut in half
1 small head Boston lettuce
2 cans tuna, drained (7-oz size)
1 onion, quartered and thinly sliced
2 ripe tomatoes, cut in wedges
2 hard-cooked eggs, quartered
1 can anchovies (2-oz size) (optional), drained
¾ c pitted ripe olives
1 tbsp capers

EQUIPMENT NEEDED

Cutting board
French and utility knives
Blender
2 large bowls
Large, shallow serving bowl or platter
Saucepan
Liquid and dry measures

PROCEDURE

1. Prepare dressing by combining all ingredients in blender and blending vigorously.
2. Pour enough salad dressing over warm potato slices and cooked beans (in separate bowls) to coat vegetables.
3. Before serving, rub inside of a salad bowl or platter with cut surface of garlic. Line bowl or a platter with lettuce.
4. Unmold tuna in center of bowl and separate into chunks.
5. Arrange separate mounds of potatoes, green beans, onion, tomatoes, and hard-cooked eggs in colorful grouping around tuna. Garnish with anchovies (optional), olives, and capers.
6. Pour dressing over all before serving.

Greek Salad

Yield: 8 servings

INGREDIENTS NEEDED

Dressing

⅓ c olive oil
¼ c wine vinegar
½ tsp salt
1 tsp oregano

Salad

1 large head romaine, torn in pieces
1 cucumber, peeled and cut in 3½-in. pieces
1 small bunch radishes, cleaned
2 small green peppers, cored
1 can (8 oz) whole beets, drained
4 tomatoes
⅓ lb feta cheese
Greek olives
Anchovy fillets (optional)

EQUIPMENT NEEDED

Cutting board
Liquid and dry measures
French knife
Paring knife
Vegetable peeler
Salad bowl for presentation
Pastry cutter

PROCEDURE

1. For salad dressing, mix all ingredients and refrigerate.
2. For salad, put romaine pieces in large salad bowl.
3. Using French knife, slice cucumber, radishes, green peppers, and beets.
4. Cut tomatoes into wedges.
5. Crumble feta cheese with hands or pastry cutter.
6. Combine prepared ingredients with romaine in bowl, sprinkle with crumbled feta cheese, and top with olives and—if desired—anchovy fillets. Pour dressing over salad and serve.

PRODUCT EVALUATION SHEET

Name _____   Lab date_____

Product prepared_____   Total prep time _____

Cooking method_____

Describe the following in one or two short sentences.

APPEARANCE (size, shape, consistency, etc.):

COLOR (golden brown, pasty white, bright, dull, etc.):

TEXTURE (smooth, lumpy, fine, coarse, sticky, gummy, etc.):

FLAVOR (sweet, sour, bitter, strong, spicy, bland, etc.):

TEMPERATURE (warm, hot, cold . . . Is it appropriate for the product?):

PROBLEMS ENCOUNTERED:

SOLUTION:
Suggestions to alter or improve the product:
1.

2.

Rating (10 being perfect):

0   1   2   3   4   5   6   7   8   9   10

20

Salad Dressings

Salad dressings are liquids or semiliquids used to enhance salads. Sometimes considered cold sauces, they serve the same functions as sauces: they flavor, moisten, and enrich.

Most of the basic salad dressings used today can be divided into three categories:

1. Oil and vinegar dressings (most unthickened dressings)
2. Mayonnaise-based dressings (most thickened dressings)
3. Cooked dressings (similar in appearance to mayonnaise dressings but more tart, and with little or no oil content)

There are also a number of dressings whose main ingredients include such products as sour cream, yogurt, and fruit juices. Many of these are designed especially for fruit salads or for low-calorie diets.

Basic Ingredients

Because the flavors of most salad dressings are not modified by cooking, their quality depends very directly on the quality of the ingredients. Most salad dressings are made primarily of an oil and an acid, with other ingredients added to modify the flavor or texture.

Oil

You can choose from a great variety of oils for your salad dressing. **Corn oil** is widely used in dressings. It has a light golden color and very little taste except for a very mild cornmeal-type flavor. **Cottonseed oil, soybean oil,** and **safflower oil** are bland, nearly flavorless oils. **Vegetable oil** or **salad oil** is a blend of oils and is popular because of its neutral flavor and relatively low cost.

Olive oil has a very distinctive, fruity flavor and aroma and a greenish color. The best olive oils are called **virgin,** which means they are made from the first pressing of the olives. Because of its flavor, olive oil is not an all-purpose oil but may be used in specialty salads such as Caesar salads. **Walnut oil** has a distinctive flavor and a high price. It is occasionally used in elegant restaurants featuring specialty salads. Other nut oils, such as hazelnut oil, are sometimes used.

Vinegar

Like oil, vinegar is available in many varieties. **Cider vinegar** is made from apples. It is brown and has a slightly sweet, appley taste. **White** or **distilled vinegar** is purified so that it has a neutral flavor.

Wine vinegar may be white or red, and it has, naturally, a winey flavor. White is preferred to red for salad dressings because red vinegar may give the dressing a muddy color. **Flavored vinegars** are modified by the addition of another product, usually tarragon or garlic. **Specialty vinegars** are used for their distinctive flavors. They include malt vinegar, sherry vinegar, raspberry vinegar, and so on. They are rarely seen in commercial kitchens.

Seasonings and Flavorings

Nearly any herb or spice can be used in salad dressings. Remember that dried herbs and spices need extra time to release their flavors if they are not heated in the product. This is why most salad dressings are best made 2 or 3 hours before serving. Other ingredients added for flavoring include mustard, catsup, Worcestershire sauce, and various kinds of cheese.

Emulsification

A uniform mixture of two normally unmixable liquids is called an **emulsion.** As you know, oil and water do not ordinarily stay mixed but separate into layers. Salad dressings, however, must be evenly mixed for proper service, even though they are made primarily of oil and vinegar. One liquid—the oil—is said to be **in suspension** in the other.

Temporary Emulsions

A simple oil and vinegar dressing is called a **temporary emulsion,** formed in the process of stirring or shaking. The harder the mixture is beaten or shaken, the longer it takes to separate. This is because the oil is broken into smaller droplets, which take longer to collect and rise to the surface. The disadvantage of oil and vinegar dressings is that they must be shaken or stirred before each use.

Permanent Emulsions

Mayonnaise is also a mixture of oil and vinegar, but the two liquids do not separate. This is because the formula also contains egg yolk, which acts as an emulsifier. The egg yolk forms a layer around each of the tiny oil droplets and holds them in suspension. Thus mayonnaise is a **permanent emulsion.** The harder the mayonnaise is beaten to break up the droplets, the more stable the emulsion becomes.

All emulsions, whether permanent or temporary, form more easily at room temperature because a chilled oil is harder to break up into small droplets.

Other emulsifying agents besides egg yolk are used in some preparations. Cooked dressings use starch in addition to eggs. Commercially made dressings may use such emulsifiers as gums, starches, and gelatin.

Types of Salad Dressing

Oil and Vinegar Dressings

Basic French dressing is a simple mixture of oil, vinegar, and seasonings. It can be used as is, but it usually serves as a base for other dressings.

The ratio of oil to vinegar in basic French dressing is 3 parts oil to 1 part vinegar. This ratio may be changed to reflect the chef's preference and the use of the dressing itself. Some chefs prefer a more oily dressing with a milder taste.

Emulsified Dressings

Emulsified French dressing is similar to basic French dressing except that egg yolk has been added to keep the oil and vinegar from separating. Its preparation is similar to that of mayonnaise. The addition of Spanish paprika gives emulsified French dressing a red-orange color and a keen flavor.

Mayonnaise is the most important emulsified dressing. It is sometimes used alone as a salad dressing, but it more often serves as the base for a wide variety of other dressings.

Mayonnaise-based dressings are generally thick and creamy. In fact, many of them are made with the addition of sour cream.

Good-quality prepared mayonnaise is readily available on the market, so few establishments make their own. Like the mother sauces we discussed in Chapter 11, it is a basic preparation and the foundation of many others. Therefore, it is important to know how to prepare it.

Homemade mayonnaise is not as stable as the commercial product, which has been beaten harder for a finer emulsion, and which may contain added stabilizers that increase its shelf life. Also, the commercial product is usually less expensive. Nevertheless, making mayonnaise in your operation takes only minutes with a power mixer, and by carefully selecting your ingredients, you can make a superior-tasting product.

Procedure for Preparing Mayonnaise

To make mayonnaise, you must observe several conditions in order to get an emulsion. Study the following steps before proceeding with the recipe at the end of the chapter.

1. Use fairly bland ingredients if the mayonnaise is to serve as a base for other dressings. Your mayonnaise will be more versatile if it has no strong flavors. Olive oil and other ingredients with distinctive flavors may be used for special preparations.
2. Have all ingredients at room temperature. Cold oil is not easily broken into small droplets, so it is harder to make an emulsion.
3. Beat the egg yolks well in a bowl. Thorough beating of the yolks is important for a good emulsion.
4. Beat in the seasonings.
    Note: Some chefs add part of the vinegar at this point because they feel it helps to disperse the spices. Others do not because they feel that a better emulsion results if they don't add vinegar until after the emulsion begins to form.

SALAD DRESSING TERMS

Acid: A salad dressing ingredient, usually a vinegar or a citrus juice

Binder: An ingredient added to a salad dressing to keep the mixture from separating

Boiled dressing: Salad dressing that is cooked

Cider vinegar: A vinegar made from fermented apple juice

Citrus fruit: Fruits such as lemons, oranges, or grapefruits

Emulsion: In a salad dressing, the condition produced when suspended particles of oil are scattered through the mixture of seasonings and acid liquid

French dressing: A temporary emulsion dressing made from oil, vinegar or citrus juice, and seasonings

Green goddess dressing: A dressing made by adding chopped green onions and anchovies to a mayonnaise base

Mayonnaise: A permanent emulsion dressing made from oil, vinegar, egg yolk, lemon juice, and seasonings

Oil: Liquid that is pressed or squeezed from the seeds or flesh of various vegetables

Permanent emulsion: A dressing in which the ingredients will not separate but will remain in suspension

Temporary emulsion: A dressing in which the ingredients will separate if the dressing is allowed to stand for a time

Thousand Island dressing: A dressing made by adding chili sauce, sweet pickle relish, and chopped hard-cooked eggs to a mayonnaise base

Vinegar: A sour, acid liquid made by fermenting fruit juices or distilled alcohol

Wine vinegar: A vinegar that is made from fermented grape juice

Yolk: The yellow part of an egg

---

5. Begin to add the oil very slowly, beating constantly. **Add the oil slowly at first, or the emulsion will break** (return to liquid).
    When the emulsion has begun to form, you may add the oil more quickly. But

never add more oil at one time than the amount of mayonnaise that has already formed in the bowl, or the emulsion may break.

6. Gradually beat in the remaining oil alternately with the vinegar. The more oil you add, the thicker the mayonnaise gets. Vinegar thins it out.

   Add a little vinegar whenever the mayonnaise gets too thick to beat. Beating with a power mixer, using the wire whip attachment, makes a more stable emulsion than beating by hand.

7. Add no more than 8 ounces of oil per large egg yolk, or 1 quart per four large egg yolks. The emulsion may break if you add more oil than the egg yolks can handle.

8. Taste and correct the seasonings. Finished mayonnaise should have a smooth and rich but neutral flavor, with a pleasant tartness. Its texture should be smooth and glossy, and it should be thick enough to hold its shape.

9. If the mayonnaise breaks, it can be rescued. Beat an egg yolk or two or some good prepared mayonnaise in a bowl, and very slowly begin to beat in the broken mayonnaise, as in step 5. Continue until all the mayonnaise has been added and re-formed.

Other Dressings

Cooked salad dressing is similar in appearance to mayonnaise, but it has a more tart, less rich flavor. Cooked dressing is made with little or no oil and with a starch thickener. It may be made in the kitchen or purchased ready prepared. Formerly it was rarely used in commercial kitchens because of its stronger flavor and tartness, but now it is preferred to mayonnaise in some foodservice operations.

In many cookbooks you will find a great variety of other dressings based neither on mayonnaise nor on oil and vinegar. They include sour cream–based dressings, fruit juice and yogurt–based dressings for fruit salads, and low-calorie dressings that appeal to the dieter. The important thing to remember is that these dressings should have well-balanced flavors with a pleasant tartness and that they should harmonize with and complement the salads with which they are served.

Mayonnaise

Yield: 1 quart

INGREDIENTS NEEDED
1 egg yolk
1 whole egg
Pinch salt
Pinch dry mustard
White pepper to taste
1 qt salad oil
⅛ c water
5 tbsp cider vinegar
Dash hot sauce

EQUIPMENT NEEDED
Electric mixer with wire whip
attachment and mixing bowl
Cup measure
Measuring spoons
Bain-marie

PROCEDURE

1. Place whole egg and yolk in mixing bowl.
2. Add salt, dry mustard, and pepper. Whip slightly.
3. Add half of oil, pouring in a very slow stream with mixer running at high speed, to form emulsion.
4. Add water, vinegar, hot sauce, and remaining oil alternately, one-third at a time.
5. Check seasoning. Pour into bain-marie and refrigerate.

Precautions

1. When adding oil, pour in a very slow stream or emulsion will not form. After emulsion has formed, continue to pour slowly because there is still a chance it may break.
2. Have electric mixer running at high speed throughout entire operation.

Blue Cheese–Sour Cream Dressing

Yield: 1 quart

INGREDIENTS NEEDED

1½ c mayonnaise
1½ c sour cream
2 tbsp dry mustard
2 tbsp lemon juice
¼ c onion, minced
2 tbsp chives, minced
1 c blue cheese, chopped

EQUIPMENT NEEDED

Cup measure
Spoon measure
Bain-marie
French knife
Kitchen spoon
Wire whip
Cutting board

PROCEDURE

1. Place mayonnaise, sour cream, dry mustard, and lemon juice in bain-marie and whip until smooth.
2. Fold in onions, chives, and blue cheese.
3. Check seasoning and place in cooler until ready for use.

Precautions

1. Soften dry mustard in the lemon juice before adding it to the other ingredients.
2. Freeze the blue cheese before chopping for best results.

Honey Dressing

Yield: 1 quart

INGREDIENTS NEEDED

1 c honey
1 c sugar
2 tsp salt
2 tsp paprika
3 tsp dry mustard
3 tsp celery seed
½ tsp white pepper
1 c lemon juice
2 c salad oil

EQUIPMENT NEEDED

Cup measure
Spoon measure
Wire whip
Bain-marie

PROCEDURE

1. Have all equipment and ingredients handy.
2. Place all ingredients in bain-marie and whip by hand until blended thoroughly.
3. Refrigerate in cooler until ready for use.

Precaution

Stir and shake well before serving.

Vinaigrette Dressing

Yield: 1 quart

INGREDIENTS NEEDED

1 pt cider vinegar
1 pt salad oil
1 tsp sugar
1 tsp white pepper
1 tbsp parsley, chopped
1 tbsp chives, minced
1 tbsp green olives, chopped fine
1 tbsp capers, chopped fine
1 hard-cooked egg, chopped fine
1 tbsp sweet pickles, chopped fine
1 tbsp pimentos, chopped fine

EQUIPMENT NEEDED

Cutting board
Quart measure
Spoon measure
Kitchen spoon or ladle
Bain-marie
French knife

PROCEDURE

1. Have all equipment and ingredients handy.
2. Combine vinegar, oil, sugar, and pepper, mixing briskly.
3. Place all ingredients in bain-marie and blend thoroughly.
4. Place in cooler until ready for use.

Boiled or Cooked Dressing

Boiled or cooked dressing is used with items that require a certain degree of tartness such as cole slaw, potato salad, and some fruit salads.

Yield: 2 quarts

INGREDIENTS NEEDED

10 whole eggs
1 c flour
½ c sugar
2 tbsp salt
3 tbsp dry mustard
1½ qt milk
10 oz cider vinegar
½ c butter or margarine

EQUIPMENT NEEDED

Quart measure
Cup measure
Spoon measure
Double boiler
Wire whip
Bain-marie

PROCEDURE

1. Break eggs.
2. Place eggs in top of double boiler.
3. Add flour, sugar, salt, and dry mustard. Blend together.
4. Add the milk and whip until mixture is smooth.
5. Drip vinegar in slowly.
6. Cook in the double boiler, whipping constantly, until mixture is thickened and smooth.
7. Remove from heat; whip in butter or margarine.
8. Pour into bain-marie. Let cool and refrigerate in cooler until ready for use.

Precaution

Whip mixture constantly while cooking to ensure a smooth dressing.

Thick French Dressing

Yield: 2 quarts

INGREDIENTS NEEDED
½ c lemon juice
½ pt cider vinegar
3 tbsp paprika
1½ tsp salt
½ c sugar
1½ tsp Worcestershire sauce
2 dashes hot sauce
¼ c catsup
¼ tsp dry mustard
1 whole egg
2 qt salad oil

EQUIPMENT NEEDED
Electric mixer with whip attachment
Quart measure
Bain-marie
Spoon measure

PROCEDURE

1. Blend together lemon juice, vinegar, paprika, salt, sugar, Worcestershire sauce, hot sauce, catsup, and dry mustard.
2. Place egg in mixing bowl. Beat at high speed with electric mixer.
3. Pour oil in a very slow stream while continuing to beat at high speed.
4. As emulsion forms and mixture thickens, add the above mixture (step 1) to thin it down. Continue this process until all ingredients are incorporated.
5. Check seasonings. Pour into bain-marie and refrigerate in cooler.

Precautions

1. When adding oil pour in a very slow stream, or emulsion will not form. After emulsion has formed, continue to pour slowly because there is still a chance it may break.
2. Operate electric mixer at high speed at least until half the oil is added.

PRODUCT EVALUATION SHEET

Name _____   Lab date_____

Product prepared_____   Total prep time _____

Cooking method_____

Describe the following in one or two short sentences.

APPEARANCE (size, shape, consistency, etc.):

COLOR (golden brown, pasty white, bright, dull, etc.):

TEXTURE (smooth, lumpy, fine, coarse, sticky, gummy, etc.):

FLAVOR (sweet, sour, bitter, strong, spicy, bland, etc.):

TEMPERATURE (warm, hot, cold . . . Is it appropriate for the product?):

PROBLEMS ENCOUNTERED:

SOLUTION:
Suggestions to alter or improve the product:
1.

2.

Rating (10 being perfect):

0   1   2   3   4   5   6   7   8   9   10

21

Yeast Breads

Classes of Yeast Breads

Yeast products exist in wide variety. They can be classified according to the kinds of flour they are made from, such as whole wheat and rye, or according to their forms or shapes, such as loaf breads, rolls, and doughnuts.

Loaf Breads

The most common yeast products are the loaf breads. They include the plain breads that are known, according to their flour content, as white, whole wheat, cracked wheat, and rye. Some variations of basic white bread are raisin, cinnamon, and nut breads. Breads made from sweetened yeast doughs may be fashioned into tea rings and coffee cakes.

Rolls

Small pieces of yeast dough are shaped into rolls. Rolls are made from both plain and sweetened doughs and take a variety of shapes. Rolls made from plain doughs are often used instead of sliced loaf breads.

Sweet Yeast Doughs

Sweet yeast doughs are made into many varieties of fancy sweet rolls. They are frequently frosted or iced and enhanced by the addition of ingredients such as raisins, fruits, nuts, and spices.

Doughnuts

The term **doughnut** refers to dough that has been fried in deep fat. The raised doughnut is made from a yeast dough; the cake-style doughnut is made without yeast. Doughnuts are most often used as desserts or in place of sweet rolls rather than as a bread substitute.

Ingredients in Yeast Breads

Nothing quite measures up to the satisfaction and pride derived from a well-made loaf of fragrant, golden brown bread. This enjoyment and pride can be yours, too, when you begin by selecting the proper ingredients.

The basic ingredients of all yeast doughs are flour, yeast, liquid, and salt; sugar and shortening are often used. Crusty, crisp breads like French or Italian bread are made with only the four basic ingredients, whereas breads with soft crust use all the ingredients. Of course, the ingredients used will determine the characteristics of the bread.

Flour

Flour is a cereal product made by milling (grinding) the kernel of the grain. It gives structure and body to bakery products. Different kinds of flour go into the many different products that a bakeshop produces. Different kinds of grain are blended to produce the kinds of flour needed.

The flours most often used in the bakeshop are made from wheat because wheat contains the highest proportion of the proteins **gliadin** and **glutenin,** which combine to form gluten in the dough. Gluten is essential to the texture of yeast breads; we will discuss it in detail later in the chapter.

White flours are made from the starchy interior of the wheat kernel, which contains the gluten-forming proteins. There are two types of wheat, hard and soft, that yield the flours used in the bakeshop—bread flour, cake flour, and pastry flour. Each provides the particular qualities needed for different types of doughs.

Bread Flour

Bread flour is a strong flour made from hard wheat. It is capable of forming the long, strong gluten strands needed for such crusty, chewy products as French bread and hard rolls.

Cake Flour

Cake flour, on the other hand, is known as a weak flour because it is made from soft wheat, which has considerably less protein. The flour is useful in making soft, tender products such as high-quality cakes and doughnuts.

Pastry Flour

Pastry flour, another weak flour, has a slightly higher protein content. It is used in pie doughs, quick breads, muffins, biscuits, pastries, and some cookies—products that require a somewhat firmer structure than cakes.

All-Purpose Flour

A fourth familiar type of flour, all-purpose flour, is a combination of 40 percent strong and 60 percent weak flours. Because it is all-purpose, it does not serve any single purpose as well as a specific flour type, but it can be used in formulas calling for pastry flour.

Whole Wheat Flour

Whole wheat flour is milled from the entire kernel. This makes it more nutritionally complete than white flours, but it yields a heavier, denser product because its gluten is less elastic. For this

reason it is usually combined with white flour in making muffins, breads, rolls, and even pie doughs.

Flour from Other Grains

Flours made from rye, soybeans, oats, and barley are sometimes chosen for specialty items or to provide menu variety. All of these flours have protein, but it is not the gluten-forming kind. They are usually combined with a strong flour to provide gluten.

Meal

Meal, especially cornmeal, may also be used in combination with wheat flour. Meal is a cereal product that is less finely ground than flour. Cornmeal makes pleasantly coarse-textured products with a special flavor, such as cornbread, corn sticks, and muffins.

Gluten

Gluten is a protein present in wheat flours that gives structure and strength to baked goods. In order for gluten to be developed, the proteins must first absorb water. Then, as the dough or batter is mixed or kneaded, the gluten forms long, elastic strands. As the dough or batter is leavened, these strands capture the gases in tiny pockets or cells, and we say that the product "rises." In the baking process the gluten, like all proteins, coagulates or solidifies and gives structure to the product.

Flour is mostly starch, as you know, but it is the protein or gluten content—not the starch—that concerns the baker most. Without gluten proteins to give structure, baked goods would not hold together.

The baker must be able to control the gluten. For example, we want French bread to be firm and chewy; this consistency requires much gluten. On the other hand, we want cakes to be tender, which means that we want very little gluten development.

Ingredient proportions and mixing methods are determined in part by their effects on the development of gluten. The baker has several ways to adjust gluten development by the selection of proper flours.

Only wheat flour will develop gluten. To make bread from rye and other grains, the baker must balance the formula with some high-gluten flour, or the bread will be heavy.

Yeast

Yeast is a living plant that multiplies under favorable conditions, produces the gas carbon dioxide, and thereby creates light and appetizing rolls, breads, and sweet rolls from heavy doughs. Yeast also has other virtues. It increases digestibility, adds flavor, and contributes small amounts of protein, minerals, and vitamins.

The process by which yeast works is called **fermentation.** This process requires three factors:

1. The right food
2. The right amount of moisture
3. The right temperature

The right food is provided by the sugars in wheat flour and by sugar itself. Moisture comes from the liquids in the formula. The right dough temperature is 70°F to 90°F. During fermentation the yeast breaks down the sugars into carbon dioxide, alcohol, and water. The rising of the dough indicates the progress of this leavening action, which takes 1 to 3 hours.

Fermentation continues until the dough is baked. At 140°F the yeast organisms are killed, but by this time the bubbles they have made are trapped safely in a strong gluten framework. The alcohol evaporates during the baking.

There are two forms of yeast, compressed and active dry. **Compressed yeast** comes in a springy yet firm grayish cake. To add it to the dough, you dissolve it in the amount of warm liquid (twice its weight or more) specified in the formula or recipe. A temperature of 90°F to 100°F makes a good start. Compressed yeast should be stored in the cooler.

Active dry yeast is compressed yeast with the water removed. It is granulated and is either mixed with warm liquid from the formula or added to the dough with the dry ingredients. Because there are many types of dry yeast, you must follow the manufacturer's instructions carefully. Active dry yeast should be stored in a cool, dry place.

Liquid

In baking, the liquid provides the moisture needed to develop gluten and to dissolve the dry ingredients. The liquid ingredient of bread is usually milk or water or a combination of the two. Breads made with milk contain more nutrients, brown better, and are more flavorful.

Salt

Salt improves the flavor of bread and controls the rate of yeast growth. It slows the yeast growth so that fermentation is controlled and the bread will be moderately firm. Too much salt will inhibit the growth of yeast and produce a heavy bread.

Sugar

Breads can be made without sugar, but a small amount of sugar is a ready source of food for yeast and speeds up yeast activity. **Caution:** Avoid using too much sugar because this will slow down yeast action. Sugar helps the crust to brown and can contribute to flavor.

Shortening

Shortenings are hydrogenated animal or vegetable fats made especially for baking. They are practically 100 percent fat, contain no water, and have a higher melting point than either butter or margarine. There are several kinds of shortening, falling into two groups: regular and emulsified shortening.

Regular shortening has a tough, waxy texture, a bland flavor, and a high melting point. Shortenings of this class can form small particles to produce the flaky texture of pie doughs and biscuits. Because they are also good at absorbing and retaining air when creamed, they are good leavening agents. This type of shortening is the one most widely used in baking.

Emulsified shortening, also called **high-ratio shortening,** is softer than regular shortening. It emulsifies easily with other ingredients and can incorporate more air than other shortenings when used in creaming. Because it can hold ingredients together without breaking or curdling, it is used in formulas with more sugar than flour and in cakes and icings high in sugar and liquid.

Preparation of Yeast Dough

Several steps are required to make perfect yeast breads. You must use the right proportion of ingredients and combine them in the order listed in the recipe. You must knead the dough sufficiently to develop gluten and permit it to ferment properly so that enough carbon dioxide is produced. You must shape the dough correctly and bake it in the right pan at the proper temperature.

There are three basic methods for mixing dough: the straight dough method, the modified straight dough method, and the sponge dough method.

In the **straight dough method,** you place all ingredients in the mixer bowl and combine them, using the dough hook. Fermentation begins during mixing and continues until the yeast is killed when the dough temperature reaches 140°F in the oven.

Between mixing and baking, the yeast needs time to work its chemical magic. So you place the dough in a **proof box**—a special cabinet with controlled temperature and high humidity. If you do not have a proof box, you can place the dough in an oiled container, oil the surface, and cover the container to prevent crust from forming. Let the dough ferment until it has doubled in volume and does not spring back but holds an indent when you press it lightly with your fingertips. The best temperature for fermentation is about 80°F.

Punching is the next step in the straight dough method. This means pulling up the sides of the dough mass and pushing them down in the center until the dough has deflated. This equalizes the temperature, allows the gluten to relax, and redistributes the yeast so the dough will rise again.

Some rich doughs require a **modified straight dough method,** in which the ingredients are combined in installments to ensure that such ingredients as fat and sugar are completely integrated into the dough.

In the third major method, the **sponge dough method,** ingredients are mixed in two stages. In the first stage the liquid, part of the flour, and the yeast are mixed to a smooth, thick batter, or sponge, which is fermented until doubled in volume. The sponge is then mixed with the remaining flour and other ingredients to form the dough.

In the sponge method, the sponge alone is fermented. After the remaining ingredients are added, another brief fermentation usually follows. You do not punch the sponge after it ferments. Mixing in the remaining ingredients accomplishes the same purposes.

When fermentation is complete, the dough can be **scaled**—weighed into portions of the desired size. The dough is divided on the bench. You dust the surface lightly with flour, cut the dough with a dough cutter or sharp knife to avoid stretching it, and weigh it on the scale.

Rounding is a preliminary makeup technique. Your aim is to form each portion of dough into a round ball with a smooth skin that will contain the gases effectively. You use the cupped palm of your hand to roll the dough around on the bench while pressing it against the bench surface with the outside edge of your hand.

Bench proofing means fermenting at the bench. The balls of dough are covered and allowed to rest at the bench for 10 to 20 minutes as fermentation continues. This relaxes the gluten and makes makeup easier.

Makeup and panning bring you closer to the final product. Makeup means forming the dough into its final shape. The goal of this step is familiar: uniformity of size and appearance that will lead to attractive, evenly baked portions. An immense variety of shapes and sizes is possible. After makeup, bread and rolls are placed in pans or molds or properly spaced on sheet pans. Those baked on sheet pans are called **hearth breads,** from the days when they were placed directly on the oven floor or hearth for baking.

Proofing is the bakeshop term for another fermentation or leavening period distinct from the first fermentation. The best conditions for proofing are a humidity of 85 percent and a temperature of 90°F to 100°F to keep the dough at 80°F. If a proof box is not available, duplicate these conditions as closely as possible and cover the dough to retain moisture and prevent a skin from forming. Proofing is complete when the dough has doubled in volume and remains indented when pressed. **Handle with care: Raised dough is fragile and is easily deflated.**

Baking comes next. Before placing them in the oven, bakers **cut** or **dock** loaves and some rolls by slashing the top with a sharp knife. This allows for even expansion in the oven. Most products are brushed with a wash to provide shine, crispness, browning, or all three. Pans are then carefully placed in the oven. Lean doughs and small rolls bake quickly at high temperatures; rich doughs and large loaves bake at lower temperatures for a longer time.

Yeast products rise rapidly in the oven at first as gases expand. Fermentation ends as the temperature rises, and the product firms as the starches gelatinize and the proteins coagulate. The crust forms and browns. The product is done when the crust is golden brown and the loaves sound hollow when tapped lightly.

You may think of baking as the final step, but two more steps are essential to preserve that fresh-baked quality. **Cooling** allows excess moisture to escape. Products baked in molds should be removed and placed on screens or racks so that air can circulate around them. Bread and rolls baked on sheet pans can be left on the pans to cool. Keep drafts away from hot breads, or the crust may split.

Storage is the final step for all baked goods. Its goal is to inhibit **staling**—deterioration of texture and aroma caused by loss of moisture and changes in the structure of the starches.

YEAST-RAISED PRODUCT TERMS

Carbon dioxide: A gas formed by the action of yeast on the ingredients in bread dough

Compressed yeast: A moist form of yeast that must be dissolved in liquid before being used to make bread dough

Docking: The process of making cuts in the top of a bread loaf before baking it

Dough hook: An attachment used on an electric mixer to knead bread dough by machine

Dry yeast: A granular form of yeast that may be combined with other dry ingredients for mixing into bread dough

Formula: A recipe or a list of ingredients and directions for preparing a certain food item

Gluten: An elastic substance that is formed when flour and water are mixed and manipulated and that gives baked products their structural strength

Humidity: The amount of moisture in the air

Knead: To fold and press dough to develop the gluten that will give the bread its structure

Leavening agent: A gas such as air, steam, or carbon dioxide that, when trapped in a dough and heated, causes the dough to increase in volume

Pan proofing: The final rising process in which shaped loaves of bread in their baking pans are placed in a proof box and allowed to rise, usually until they have doubled in size

Proof: To raise a yeast dough by putting it in a warm, moist place

Proof box: A cabinet with temperature and humidity controls that is used to proof bread dough

Punch: To press raised dough with the fist to force out extra gases trapped during the rising process

Sheeting: In mixing dough, the point at which the dough pulls into long, flat strands

Yeast: A group of one-celled, microscopic plants that produce the leavening agent, carbon dioxide, in many baked products

Staling begins very soon after baking, but breads, rolls, biscuits, and quick breads to be served within 8 hours can be stored at room temperature. If they must be kept longer, wrap them in plastic wrap or place in plastic bags after they are thoroughly cool. If you wrap them before they cool, moisture will collect and make the breads soggy—particularly undesirable in hard-crusted goods.

Always store baked goods in the freezer. Refrigeration actually increases staling, so don't follow this common practice. Freshen frozen baked goods in the oven at a low temperature for a short time, or simply let them thaw.

Nutritional Contributions of Yeast Breads

Yeast breads are a rich source of energy and can make important contributions to meet daily nutritional needs. The nutritional value of bread is influenced by the ingredients used to make it. Flour, the chief ingredient of bread, contributes significantly to its energy value. If you use enriched and whole wheat flour in yeast breads, they will also provide thiamine or vitamin B-1, riboflavin or vitamin B-2, niacin, and iron. When milk is used instead of water, it too adds nutrients. Milk will make bread an even better food because it is a rich source of calcium, riboflavin, and complete protein. Whole milk will also supply vitamin A. Some yeast doughs are further enriched by the inclusion of eggs.

Bread is a nutritious food with a low-key flavor that blends well with many foods. For this reason, bread continues to be the staff of life and should be included in meals in a variety of ways.

Convenience in Yeast Breads

Whole loaves of baked bread, followed by sliced bread, were among the first convenience food items. Since then many new convenience items, of both the yeast bread and quick bread varieties, have been added. They include mixes as well as frozen, refrigerated, and brown-and-serve products that need only be warmed or baked. The mix for bread contains all of the measured ingredients except the liquid. Adding the liquid to the mix, stirring, and shaping the dough require little time.

There are so many varieties of convenience bread items that it becomes difficult to evaluate their quality, nutrient value, cost, and savings in time and effort. To help the consumer, the USDA has made a study of convenience items and compared them with homemade products. The study found that brown-and-serve and ready-to-serve yeast rolls were the most expensive. Frozen yeast rolls were slightly more expensive than homemade items, and homemade items were still the lowest in cost.

Convenience products will help you save time, especially when the homemade product requires many ingredients and several steps for preparation. When deciding whether or not to use convenience products, bear in mind that their only benefit is a saving in time.

You can also save time and gain convenience with frozen homemade products. Yeast doughs can be frozen for about 6 weeks, and baked products for several months. Frozen baked products are more of a convenience than frozen yeast dough, which requires thawing, shaping, rising, and baking.

Sour Cream Herb Bread

Yield: 2 loaves

INGREDIENTS NEEDED
3¼ c all-purpose flour
2 packages active dry yeast
¼ c sugar
1 tsp salt
½ tsp celery seed
½ tsp dill weed
½ tsp grated lemon peel
1 c sour cream
½ c hot tap water
3 tbsp butter or margarine
1 egg
Sesame seeds, if desired

EQUIPMENT NEEDED
Electric mixer and bowl
Liquid and dry measures
Kitchen spoon
Proof box
2 loaf pans, 8 × 4
Hand-held thermometer
Oven, preheated to 350°F

PROCEDURE

1. In large mixing bowl, blend 2 cups of flour with remaining ingredients.
2. Beat 2 minutes at medium speed.
3. By hand, stir in remaining 1¼ cups flour.
4. Cover and let rise in proof box for approximately 30 minutes.
5. Grease loaf pans.
6. Stir batter vigorously; pour into greased pans.
7. Cover and let rise again in proof box for approximately 30 minutes or until doubled in size.
8. Bake at 350°F 35 to 40 minutes or until golden brown.
9. Remove from loaf pans immediately; brush with butter or margarine and sprinkle with sesame seeds (optional).

White Bread

Yield: 2 loaves

INGREDIENTS NEEDED
2 c milk
1 package dry yeast or 1 cake compressed yeast
¼ c warm water (110°F) (use water
at 80°F for compressed yeast)
2 tbsp sugar
1½ tbsp shortening
2½ tsp salt
6 c all-purpose flour (approx.)

EQUIPMENT NEEDED
Liquid and dry measures
Hand-held thermometer
Small saucepan
Bowl
Proof box
2 loaf pans 9½ × 5¼ × 2¾
Oven, preheated to 400°F

PROCEDURE

1. Scald milk.
2. Soften yeast in warm water; let stand 5 minutes.
3. Pour scalded milk over sugar, shortening, and salt in bowl.
4. When lukewarm, blend in 1 cup flour.
5. Stir in yeast and beat well.
6. Add 3 cups flour; continue beating until smooth.
7. Beat in enough remaining flour to make a soft dough.
8. Turn onto a lightly floured surface; let stand 5 minutes.
9. Knead until smooth and elastic.
10. Place dough in greased bowl; turn to bring greased surface to top.
11. Cover; set in proof box until dough is doubled in size—approximately 30 minutes.
12. Punch down, cover, and let rise again until doubled in size.
13. Turn onto lightly floured surface. Divide dough in half; let rest for approximately 5 minutes.
14. Shape into loaves and place in greased bread pans.
15. Cover and let rise again in proof box until doubled in size.
16. Bake at 400°F for approximately 1 hour or until golden brown. Remove from pans immediately after removing from oven.

Potato Bread

Yield: 2 1-pound loaves

INGREDIENTS NEEDED

3 potatoes
1 cake compressed yeast
2 tbsp shortening
2 tbsp sugar
1 tbsp salt
6 to 6½ c sifted flour

EQUIPMENT NEEDED

Liquid and dry measures
Vegetable peeler
Saucepan
Sifter
Kitchen spoon
2 loaf pans, 8 × 4
Proof box
Paring knife
Hand-held thermometer
Oven, preheated to 375°F

PROCEDURE

1. Peel and cube potatoes. Cover with water and simmer until tender.
2. Mash potatoes in liquid. Reserve ¼ cup.
3. Crumble yeast in ¼ cup of reserved liquid.
4. To remaining liquid add shortening, sugar, and salt.
5. Add softened yeast and half of flour.
6. Beat; add remaining flour gradually.
7. Knead on floured board until thoroughly elastic.
8. Place in greased bowl, cover, and place in proof box for approximately 1 hour.
9. When doubled in size, divide in 2 parts, shape into loaves, and place in greased pans.
10. Place in proof box and let rise again until doubled in size.
11. Bake at 375°F for 45 minutes or until bread shrinks away from sides of pans. Remove from pans immediately after removing from oven.

Tomato Bread

Yield: 1 loaf

INGREDIENTS NEEDED	EQUIPMENT NEEDED
1 c tomato juice	*Liquid and dry measures*
1 tbsp shortening	*Hand-held thermometer*
1 tsp salt	*1 loaf pan, 9½ × 4½*
1½ tbsp sugar	*Mixing bowl*
½ cake yeast	*Pastry brush*
¼ c lukewarm water	*Small saucepan*
3¾ c sifted all-purpose flour	*Oven, preheated to 400°F*

PROCEDURE

1. Scald tomato juice.
2. Add shortening, salt, and sugar to hot tomato juice. Cool to lukewarm.
3. Soften yeast in lukewarm water.
4. Add to cooled tomato juice mixture.
5. Add half the flour, beat until smooth, add remaining flour, and mix well.
6. Knead on floured board about 5 minutes.
7. Place in proof box until doubled in bulk, approximately 1 hour.
8. Shape into loaf, place in greased pan, and brush top with melted shortening.
9. Let rise until doubled in bulk. Bake in hot oven (400°F) for 15 minutes, then reduce heat to moderate (375°F) and bake about 45 minutes longer until golden brown and pulling away from sides of pan.

Cottage Cheese Rolls

Yield: 2 dozen

INGREDIENTS NEEDED

Rolls

2 cakes yeast
½ c warm water
5 c all-purpose flour
½ c sugar
1½ tsp salt
1 c butter
1½ lb cottage cheese

Filling

1½ c brown sugar
½ c butter
1 tsp cinnamon

EQUIPMENT NEEDED

Liquid and dry measures
Large bowl
Sifter
Pastry cutter
Large baking sheet
Parchment paper
Oven, preheated to 375°F

PROCEDURE

1. Dissolve yeast in water.
2. Sift dry ingredients into bowl.
3. Cut in butter until dough has consistency of very coarse cornmeal.
4. Blend in cottage cheese, eggs, and dissolved yeast.
5. When well mixed, turn dough onto a floured board, shape into a ball, and let it rest for 10 minutes.
6. Blend filling ingredients until crumbly.
7. Roll dough into a rectangle.
8. Sprinkle with filling, and roll as for a jelly roll.
9. Cut into 1-inch slices.
10. Place slices, cut side down, on baking sheet lined with parchment paper.
11. Let rise again until rolls have doubled in size, approximately 45 to 60 minutes.
12. Bake at 375°F for 20 minutes or until lightly brown.

Brown Sugar Doughnuts

Yield: 3 dozen

INGREDIENTS NEEDED

2 c milk
1 c brown sugar
⅔ c butter
1 cake yeast
4 eggs
1 tsp salt
4½ to 5 c all-purpose flour

EQUIPMENT NEEDED

Liquid and dry measures
Saucepan
Pastry cutter
Large bowl
Doughnut cutter
French fryer
Tongs

PROCEDURE

1. Set fryer to 375°F.
2. Scald milk.
3. Pour scalded milk over brown sugar and butter.
4. Cool until lukewarm, then stir in yeast.
5. Beat in eggs and salt.
6. Add flour gradually to make dough soft but not quite sticky.
7. Let dough rise once until doubled.
8. Roll dough on a floured board to a thickness of ½ inch.
9. Cut with a floured cutter, and let rise until doubled in size.
10. Carefully lift doughnuts off board and drop into hot deep fat (375°F).
11. Fry until browned, turning several times with tongs.

PRODUCT EVALUATION SHEET

Name _____   Lab date _____

Product prepared _____   Total prep time _____

Cooking method _____

Describe the following in one or two short sentences.

APPEARANCE (size, shape, consistency, etc.):

COLOR (golden brown, pasty white, bright, dull, etc.):

TEXTURE (smooth, lumpy, fine, coarse, sticky, gummy, etc.):

FLAVOR (sweet, sour, bitter, strong, spicy, bland, etc.):

TEMPERATURE (warm, hot, cold . . . Is it appropriate for the product?):

PROBLEMS ENCOUNTERED:

SOLUTION:
Suggestions to alter or improve the product:
1.

2.

Rating (10 being perfect):

0   1   2   3   4   5   6   7   8   9   10

22

Quick Breads

Types of Quick Breads

Quick breads are flour mixtures of many varieties that differ greatly in flavor, size, shape, and general appearance. Some quick breads are baked in an oven or on a griddle; others are deep-fried. All can be made quickly and served hot.

The quick breads are conveniently grouped according to the consistency of the batter used: pour batter, drop batter, or soft dough. The thickness or stiffness of the dough depends upon the amount of liquid used in relation to the flour. Those with less liquid are stiffer than those with more liquid.

Pour batters are thin and can be poured from the mixing bowl. They may contain the same amount of liquid as flour or slightly less liquid than flour (1 cup flour to 1 or ¾ cup liquid). Waffles, pancakes, and popovers are examples of quick breads made from pour batters.

Drop batters are fairly thick and need to be scraped from the spoon or the bowl into the baking pan. They usually contain about twice as much flour as liquid (1 cup flour to ½ cup liquid). Muffins, biscuits, and some quick loaf breads and coffee cakes are examples of quick breads made from drop batters.

Soft dough is thick enough to roll and shape by hand. It contains about one-third as much liquid as flour (1 cup flour to ⅓ or ½ cup liquid). Biscuits, doughnuts, scones, and some

quick coffee cakes are quick breads made from soft doughs.

True to their name, quick breads are made quickly and usually baked as soon as mixed. The range and varied proportions of ingredients account in part for the wide variety of quick breads.

Ingredients in Quick Breads

All quick breads, regardless of type, contain the basic ingredients of flour, leavening, salt, and liquid. In addition to these basic ingredients, shortening, egg, and sugar are frequently used. Each ingredient has a specific purpose and contributes a particular characteristic to the bread.

Flour

Flour contains the materials that form the structure or body of the bread. All-purpose flour is used most often for making quick breads.

When water is mixed with flour, gluten is formed from the protein in the flour, as discussed in the previous chapter. Gluten gives the batter or dough strength and elasticity and helps retain the air, steam, or carbon dioxide that makes the bread increase in volume.

Cornmeal, whole wheat flour, and other flours are used in some recipes for flavor and variety.

Salt

Small amounts of salt are used to improve the flavor of quick breads.

Leavening

Leavening agents enable the quick bread to rise so that it becomes light and porous. Baking powder is the most common leavening agent used in quick breads, but air, steam, and a combination of soda and acid are sometimes used. Baking powder and soda plus an acid such as sour milk or buttermilk are chemical leaveners that produce carbon dioxide, which expands in the oven and causes the bread to rise as it bakes.

Baking powders are grouped as single action (fast-acting) and double action (slow-acting). **Single-action** baking powder releases its carbon dioxide as soon as it comes in contact with liquid or moisture. **Double-action** baking powder requires both moisture and heat to release completely all of its carbon dioxide. You need to work quickly when using a single-action baking powder so that all of the carbon dioxide is not lost before the product is baked.

All baking powders are made of soda, a dry acidic powder, and cornstarch. The soda component reacts with the acid component to form carbon dioxide. Instead of baking powder, some recipes use baking soda and buttermilk or sour milk, which provides the acid required to form carbon dioxide.

Liquid

Liquid provides some of the leavening action as it is converted into steam. (When you beat air into eggs, it too can expand when heated and provide for some leavening action.) The liquid will dissolve the dry ingredients, salt, sugar, and chemical leaveners.

Milk is the liquid most often used in quick breads. However, sour milk or buttermilk is used in some recipes. Milk contributes to the flavor and browning quality of bread. You may replace homogenized milk with evaporated or dry milk. You must reconstitute evaporated milk before use by adding an equal amount of water. You may reconstitute dry milk to a liquid by following the directions on the package, or you may add it to the dry ingredients and then add water (in the amount specified for milk) to replace the fluid milk in the recipe.

Sugar

Sugar contributes to sweetness and to the golden brown color of the crust. White, granulated sugar is most commonly used, but brown sugar is used sometimes because of its richer flavor.

Fat or Shortening

Fat or shortening gives tenderness to the bread. Vegetable shortening and lard are bland in flavor, but margarine and butter contribute a pleasing flavor.

Eggs

Eggs contribute to color, texture, and nutritive value.

Nutritional Contributions of Quick Breads

The ingredients you use to make quick breads will determine their nutritional value. Flour is the basic and predominant ingredient of all quick breads. All kinds of flour are rich in starch and will thus help meet energy needs. In addition to starch, whole grain and enriched flours contribute B vitamins and iron.

Milk and eggs are rich sources of nutrients and, when used in quick breads, will increase the mineral and vitamin content and provide some complete protein. Fat and sugar add to the bread's caloric value, whereas salt and leavening make no nutritional contribution.

Uses of Quick Breads

Quick breads are versatile foods that lend themselves to a variety of uses. For example, griddle cakes (pancakes) and waffles are often featured as an entrée at breakfast, lunch, or even dinner. You may serve them with the traditional syrup and butter, or you may top them with some type of meat or poultry.

The quick loaf breads come in many flavors (raisin, nut, banana, and others) and may be used for many different preparations, including sandwiches for hors d'oeuvres. They may serve as the breadstuff to complement the main course of any meal.

Muffins and biscuits are popular hot breads that add a special touch to any meal or entrée. They are often used to garnish or accompany a main dish. Drop biscuits may appear as dumplings in a stew, and rolled biscuits may form the pastry for a meat pie.

Quick breads are also found on the dessert table. Baked, sweetened biscuits are a base for shortcake desserts. The sweetened dough may be used as the pastry for cobblers, fruit turnovers, and deep-dish pies. Waffles or pancakes topped with sweetened fruits are also served as desserts.

Principles and Preparation of Quick Breads

The success of your quick breads depends upon the kinds and proportions of ingredients you use and the way you combine them.

Flour is the chief ingredient in all quick breads. In addition to a high proportion of starch, flour also contains the proteins **gliadin** and **glutenin.** When you mix flour with water, these two proteins yield **gluten,** an elastic substance that forms a mesh-like structure in the dough or batter that can surround the gases, air, or steam responsible for leavening. The gluten will stretch as the gas expands until the heat of the oven coagulates the gluten, forming a fairly firm, porous structure.

The principles of quick bread preparation are concerned with gluten formation. When you overmix and handle a quick bread mixture too much, a large amount of gluten is developed and the bread becomes tough. **Quick breads require very little mixing and careful handling to avoid overproduction of gluten.** You will use one of two methods to mix quick breads: the biscuit method (also called the pastry method) or the muffin method.

The Biscuit Method

1. Measure or weigh all ingredients accurately.
2. Sift the dry ingredients together into a mixing bowl.
3. Cut in the shortening, using a pastry blender or the paddle on an electric mixer. Continue until the mixture resembles coarse cornmeal.

   Biscuits may be prepared in advance up to this point. Portions of each mixture may then be scaled and combined just before baking.
4. Combine all the liquid ingredients.
5. Add the liquid to the dry ingredients. Mix just until the ingredients are combined and a soft dough is formed. Do not overmix.
6. Bring the dough to the bench and knead it lightly by pressing it out and folding it in half. Rotate the dough 90° after each fold.
7. Repeat this procedure about 10 to 20 times or about 30 seconds. The dough should be soft and slightly elastic but not sticky. Overkneading toughens biscuits. The dough is now ready for makeup.
8. Roll the biscuit dough out into a sheet about ½ inch thick, being careful to roll it evenly and to a uniform thickness. (Biscuits will approximately double in height during baking.)
9. Cut into desired shapes. With round hand cutters, cutting straight down produces the best shape after baking. Do not twist the cutter. Space the cuts closely to minimize scraps. Cutting in squares or triangles with a pastry cutter or knife eliminates scraps that would have to be rerolled. Roller cut-

ters also eliminate or reduce scraps. Reworked scraps will be tougher.

10. Place the biscuits on a baking sheet, ½ inch apart for crisp-crusted biscuits or touching one another for softer biscuits. Bake as soon as possible. If desired, brush the tops with egg wash or milk before baking to aid browning.

The Muffin Method

This mixing method is used not only for muffins but also for pancakes, waffles, quick loaf breads, and coffee cakes. Loaf breads and coffee cakes are generally higher in fat and sugar than muffins, so they can withstand more mixing without toughening.

1. Thoroughly combine the dry ingredients. Sifting them together is best, but sifting can be omitted if mixing is thorough.
2. Combine all remaining ingredients, including melted fat or oil.
3. Add the liquids to the dry ingredients and mix just until all the flour is moistened. The batter will look lumpy. **Do not overmix.**
4. Pan and bake immediately. The dry and liquid mixtures may be prepared in advance. But once they are combined, the batter should be baked without delay, or loss of volume may result.
5. When portioning batter into muffin tins, be careful not to stir the mix and toughen it. Scoop the batter from the outside edge outward for best results.

The following chart outlines the two basic methods for mixing quick breads.

Care and Storage of Quick Breads

Because quick breads lose their freshness rapidly, you should store them in moistureproof wrap or in a tightly sealed container. The texture and flavor of quick breads deteriorate rapidly even under ideal storage conditions.

The freshness of quick breads is better preserved by frozen storage. Breads to be frozen should be packaged in suitable freezer wrap soon after baking. Frozen quick breads are a convenience and need only be warmed for serving.

Convenience in Quick Breads

A wide variety of convenience quick breads are available: ready-to-serve, frozen, refrigerated, and mixes. Most mixes require only the addition of milk or water; some may require eggs. The frozen or refrigerated product may require baking or simply heating.

Convenience quick bread items usually cost more than the homemade product. The frozen quick breads tend to be more expensive than the dry mixes; homemade ones are least expensive.

You may want to keep convenience quick bread mixes on hand for emergencies. In deciding which convenience item to use, you should consider the quality of the mix, the comparative cost, the time involved, and how the preparation will fit into your situation.

METHODS FOR MIXING QUICK BREADS

BISCUIT METHOD
1. Combine dry ingredients and cut in fat.
2. Combine liquid ingredients.
3. Add liquid to dry ingredients and mix just until combined.
4. If required, knead very lightly.

MUFFIN METHOD
1. Combine dry ingredients.
2. Combine liquid ingredients, including melted fat.
3. Add liquid to dry ingredients and mix just until combined.

Apple Muffins

Yield: 2 dozen

INGREDIENTS NEEDED
¼ c soft butter
⅓ c sugar
1 egg, beaten
2½ c sifted cake flour or bread flour
½ tsp salt
4 tsp baking powder
1 c milk
1 c apple, peeled and diced

EQUIPMENT NEEDED
Liquid and dry measures
Wire whip
Muffin baking pans
Sifter
Large bowl
Spatula
Ice cream scoop
Vegetable peeler
Paring knife
Oven, preheated to 400°F

PROCEDURE

1. Soak apple in light lemon-water solution.
2. Cream butter and sugar with wire whip.
3. When mixture is light and fluffy, add beaten egg.
4. Sift dry ingredients together.
5. Add dry mixture to sugar mixture alternately with milk.
6. Fold in apple and fill greased muffin tins two-thirds full, using spatula and ice cream scoop.
7. Sprinkle with sugar and cinnamon, and bake at 400°F for approximately 25 minutes.

Do not overmix batter. Batter should have the consistency of very moist cornmeal.

Standard Baking Powder Biscuits

Yield: 1 dozen

INGREDIENTS NEEDED
2 c all-purpose flour
3 tsp baking powder
½ tsp salt
¼ c butter
⅓ c milk
2 large eggs, lightly beaten

EQUIPMENT NEEDED
Liquid and dry measures
Pastry blender
Kitchen spoon
Rolling pin
Circle cutter
Baking sheet
Parchment paper
Oven, preheated to 450°F

PROCEDURE

1. Combine flour, baking powder, and salt.
2. Cut in butter with pastry blender.
3. When mixture is the consistency of coarse cornmeal, stir in liquid ingredients, using enough that dough holds together and can be kneaded.
4. Turn dough onto floured work table and knead lightly. **Do not knead more than 10 times.**
5. Roll out to a thickness of approximately ½ inch.
6. Cut into 2-inch rounds using circle cutter.
7. Place on baking sheet with parchment paper.
8. Bake at 450°F for 12 to 15 minutes.

Caution: Do not overknead the dough—if overkneaded, biscuits will be tough and very grainy!

Orange Popovers

Yield: 1 dozen

INGREDIENTS NEEDED
2 c all-purpose flour
½ tsp salt
2 tsp sugar
3 large eggs
1 c milk
1 tbsp grated orange rind
1 c orange juice
3 tbsp butter

EQUIPMENT NEEDED
Liquid and dry measures
Sifter
Large bowl
Wire whip
Muffin tins
Oven, preheated to 400°F

PROCEDURE

1. Sift the dry ingredients into large mixing bowl.
2. Beat eggs and add milk, orange rind, and juice, mixing with wire whip.
3. Pour mixture into dry ingredients.
4. Beat thoroughly.
5. Pour into buttered muffin tins, half full.
6. Bake at 400°F for 35 to 40 minutes.

Caution: Keep oven door closed at all times. Do not check popovers until they have been in the oven for a minimum of 35 minutes.

Banana Nut Bread

Yield: 1 loaf

INGREDIENTS NEEDED
½ c butter
1 c brown sugar
2 large eggs
2 c all-purpose flour
½ tsp salt
½ tsp soda
1½ c mashed bananas
½ c chopped walnuts

EQUIPMENT NEEDED
Wire whip
Mixing bowl
Liquid and dry measures
Loaf baking pan
Cutting board
French knife
Oven, preheated to 350°F

PROCEDURE

1. Cream butter and sugar with wire whip.
2. Add eggs and beat well.
3. Combine dry ingredients and stir into creamed mixture alternately with mashed bananas.
4. Fold in nuts last.
5. Pour into a buttered loaf pan. Let stand at room temperature for 20 minutes.
6. Bake at 350°F for 45 minutes to 1 hour.

Sweet Potato Doughnuts

Yield: 2–3 dozen

INGREDIENTS NEEDED

5 c all-purpose flour
7 tsp baking powder
1½ c warm mashed sweet potatoes
1 tsp salt
3 large eggs
2 c granulated sugar
2 tbsp melted butter
1 tsp nutmeg
1 c milk

EQUIPMENT NEEDED

Liquid and dry measures
Sifter
Kitchen spoon
Spatula
Vegetable peeler
Saucepan
Doughnut cutter
Tongs
Rolling pin
French fryer

PROCEDURE

1. Preheat fryer to 375°F.
2. Sift flour and baking powder.
3. Whip potatoes; gradually add salt, eggs, sugar, melted butter, nutmeg, and milk, and blend thoroughly.
4. Stir in flour and mix until well blended into a soft dough, as for biscuits.
5. Chill well for at least 1 hour.
6. Turn a portion of dough onto a floured work surface and roll or pat to a thickness of ½ inch. **Dough should be soft but firm enough that it doesn't stick to the board.**
7. Cut with floured doughnut cutter, and drop in 375°F fat.
8. Turn doughnuts as they brown.
9. Drain well and sprinkle with powdered sugar. Doughnuts are best when served hot.

French Crepes

Yield: 20

INGREDIENTS NEEDED

Crepes

2 c all-purpose flour
½ c sugar
5 large eggs
¾ c cream (half-and-half)
2 c milk
2 tbsp brandy
3 tbsp melted butter

Filling

2 lb fresh bananas
¼ c brown sugar
½ c rum
¼ c vegetable oil

EQUIPMENT NEEDED

Sifter
Wire whip
5- or 6-in. omelet pan or skillet
Liquid and dry measures
Large mixing bowl
Baking dish

PROCEDURE

1. Sift flour and sugar into mixing bowl.
2. Beat eggs with wire whip until light and pour them in bowl.
3. Add remaining ingredients and beat until smooth.
4. Let batter stand for at least 20 minutes.
5. Melt 1 teaspoon butter in skillet.
6. Pour in about ¼ cup of batter, tilting pan so that batter covers bottom.

Note: Crepes baked in the skillet do not need turning because the batter is so thin.

FILLING

1. Sauté bananas in vegetable oil until slightly brown.
2. Put half a fried banana in center of each crepe.
3. Roll up crepes and place seam side down in baking dish.
4. Sprinkle liberally with brown sugar.
5. Flame with rum.

PRODUCT EVALUATION SHEET

Name _____   Lab date _____

Product prepared_____   Total prep time _____

Cooking method_____

Describe the following in one or two short sentences.

APPEARANCE (size, shape, consistency, etc.):

COLOR (golden brown, pasty white, bright, dull, etc.):

TEXTURE (smooth, lumpy, fine, coarse, sticky, gummy, etc.):

FLAVOR (sweet, sour, bitter, strong, spicy, bland, etc.):

TEMPERATURE (warm, hot, cold . . . Is it appropriate for the product?):

PROBLEMS ENCOUNTERED:

SOLUTION:
Suggestions to alter or improve the product:
1.

2.

Rating (10 being perfect):

0   1   2   3   4   5   6   7   8   9   10

Recipe Index

Subject Index